TITANIC

The Edith Brown Story

David Haisman

authorHOUSE®

AuthorHouse™ UK Ltd.
500 Avebury Boulevard
Central Milton Keynes, MK9 2BE
www.authorhouse.co.uk
Phone: 08001974150

First published by AuthorHouse 7/15/2009

ISBN: 978-1-4389-6182-8 (sc)
ISBN: 978-1-4389-8584-8 (hc)

This book is printed on acid-free paper.

ACKNOWLEDGEMENTS

For my wife, Lyn

Also for David, Andrew, Janina, and Janette

PREFACE

To fully understand what the crew of the *Titanic* was up against, it's important to understand not only the work practices involved, but also the equipment they had to work with.

In my experience, lifeboats, davits, and boat drills are not the seaman's favourite pastime, but they are nevertheless fully realised as a necessary evil. The presence of lifeboats on all ships is reassuring to those who sail the seven seas; without them, no one would step on board a ship for neither love nor money. However, throughout a ship's lifespan of around thirty-odd years, they might never be used. Their upkeep and maintenance, and the deck space they take up, can be an expensive headache to many ship owners. Perhaps this was on the minds of those who allowed the *Titanic* to sail well short of the necessary lifeboat requirement. They might well have sailed with even less, had there not been a Board of Trade directive in force at the time, although it was totally inadequate.

Regarding a lifeboat's usefulness other than as a standby for abandoning ship, some coastal craft and cargo ships utilise the odd lifeboat for waterline paint jobs and over-the-side jobs such as rubs and scrapes by tugboat fenders, boot topping, and plimsoll line work. As long as the boats aren't at risk of damage, it's a good idea to get them into the water, apart from boat drills, to familiarise the crew with working some of the gear. However, it's fair to say that in all probability, most lifeboats have never saved a life from builder's yard to breaker's yard.

Throughout my seagoing career, covering the 1950s, '60s, and '70s, I sailed on a wide range of ships, which included ocean liners, troop ships, tankers, cargo ships, coasters, cross-channel ferries, hydrofoils, mud hoppers, and dredgers. During that time, it became clear by working with the many different types of lifeboats and davits that the Welwyn davits were one of the most labour-intensive, and Welwyn davits were used on the *Titanic*. The davits varied depending on the size of the vessel, with smaller versions being found on many coasters, tug boats, and small craft. The biggest were found on ocean liners, and those required experience and quite a bit of teamwork. As a result, Welwyn davits were used at the Southampton Lifeboat Training School in Southampton's Old Docks. It was there that we trained for our Board of Trade lifeboat certificate.

This training was a direct result of the *Titanic* disaster, as it was clear that many seamen had not had enough experience in handling these davits. Most of this gear and training should have applied to the *Titanic* era. It was also applicable to many later vessels, and the teamwork was invaluable. The problem with White Star Line and, later, Cunard White Star, was their preference for signing on many ex-servicemen and ratings unfamiliar with merchant navy work practices. This was certainly the case with other passenger liner companies as well. I can only assume that this might have been because of the ex-servicemen's past training in discipline and their willingness to wear uniforms on passenger ships. By way of current advances in the design of ships and shipboard technology, this might not necessarily apply today, but at the turn of the last century and right up until the early '60s, there were still many ships that had work practices similar to those on the *Titanic*.

Those trained in the navy would be the first to admit that warships just didn't carry the dozens of Welwyn davits and the hundreds of men, women, and children that needed to be organised in an abandon-ship operation. Many seamen at the turn of the last century were trained in sail and would have been excellent seamen in their own right, but they would have required training as new gear was introduced. Indeed, many merchant seamen were caught out on the *Titanic* that night after becoming involved in the ship's hopeless abandon-ship procedure.

The merchant seaman is in the business of selling his labour to the ship owner and is required to know his job with the minimum of fuss and basic disciplinary measures. Any seaman who doesn't know his job would certainly be unpopular with his shipmates. There just aren't enough seamen signed on to carry another who can't do his job. In my opinion, it's always a mistake by commentators to compare the merchant service to the Royal Navy, the US Navy, or any other navy, as this is totally misleading of the work ethic. The merchant seaman as I knew him was a free spirit, and not a great lover of bull. He was proud of his prowess as a seaman and his ability to serve on any merchantman afloat. There's no doubt in my mind that seamen at both the U.S. and British inquiries into the *Titanic* closed ranks in order to safeguard future work prospects for themselves and their shipmates.

When I went to sea in the early 1950s, ex-service personnel recruited into the British merchant service were encouraged to train for their able seaman's certificate, and also for the Board of Trade's Life boatman's certificate. This was not necessarily a seamanship issue for many; it was more to get people familiarised with the work practices and gear on board a merchant ship. The biggest surprise to many joining the merchant navy was how few qualified seamen there were as opposed to a naval ship.

It's quickly realised that the commercial ship owner will never sign on one more body than is absolutely necessary. This is never in question until a ship founders, and then there is the stark realisation that there are not enough qualified seamen to carry out an efficient abandon-ship procedure.

When National Service ended in Britain, the merchant navy lost a huge number of professional seamen who chose to take up work ashore. The reason for this, up until that time, was that if a seaman left the merchant navy before the age of 26, he would automatically get his call-up papers to join the army or one of the other armed forces. This, in turn, left a vacuum in the Board of Trade's existing standards for manning the huge transatlantic liners. Ship owners, with a powerful lobby in Parliament, managed to get a new type of deck rating to sign on articles within the service, and those people were known as DHUs (deck hands un-certificated). The seamen's union of the day was opposed to these changes. Some ship owners argued that these great liners could go to sea with less qualified seamen; the remainder of the crew, if necessary, could be made up of farmers.

Many in the industry were astounded at such suggestions, and to see that the lessons from the *Titanic* were being so conveniently forgotten when it suited. To refer back to the *Titanic*, and to the question of lifeboats not getting away as quickly as they could have, we have to look again at the shortage of qualified seamen handling the situation. To help the reader to understand the workings of a typical Welwyn davit, I have drawn a sketch of the set up to give some idea of what's involved in getting boats away. Ideally, to safely prepare and launch a boat with this gear, three or four qualified seamen are required, with one of them supervising as well confronting a deck full of passengers. At this time, we should remember that deck officers are required in many places at once when an abandon-ship procedure is being carried out. They are not necessarily supervising the clearing away and lowering of boats. On ocean liners at that time, there were far more lifeboats than there were deck officers, so this should have been the duty of qualified seamen, who would probably have handled the situation quite well if there had been enough of them to do so.

They would have been taking off boat covers and strong backs, releasing and clearing gripes (wires or ropes to secure the boat to the deck), and generally preparing and clearing away falls for lowering. This would have allowed two or three men to 'sweat back' (lift) on the falls in order to float the boat in readiness for swinging it out and lowering it to boat-deck level. In my experience, all lifeboats supported by Welwyn davits on the big ships in those days had to be lifted up from the chocks before swinging out, even after the tumblers (clamps holding the keel in place when stowed) had been released. Only then could two men on each handle start to wind the boat out, sometimes with the help of 'humpers' (crewmen helping to push the boat out).

Once they got a good winding momentum going, then just one man at each end could continue, as long as they observed the brass worm at each end. This was a good indicator to prevent the boat from skewing (one end going out quicker than the other). This would mean that one end had become extremely difficult for one man to continue winding out on his own. When experienced crews are carrying out these procedures, they will be aware of the snags that can arise and will ensure that the whole procedure doesn't become unnecessary hard work.

If a ship is listing, then problems are compounded. Boats being lowered on the high side (the side opposite the list) will have a tendency to snag up on all shipside protrusions such as shell door hinges, port cowls, gangway fitments, and lugs. In later years, but not on the *Titanic,* skates were fitted to all lifeboats. This was to help the boat slide down the ship's side without any real problems of getting caught up. They were considered one of the better ideas when abandoning ship, as a vessel seldom sinks on an even keel.

With a ship listing, lifeboats on the low side will have a tendency to 'drift' (go straight down) away from the ship's side as the ship goes lower, so bowsing in lines or tackles are needed to keep the boat alongside for disembarkation. If the list is pronounced, the davits should not be wound out too far in order to keep the boat further inboard for disembarkation of passengers. I doubt if this would have been necessary on the *Titanic* with a slight list of around 5 degrees, but it doesn't take a great list to begin to cause these problems.

Once a lifeboat is clear for lowering, the correct lowering hitch for the falls is applied to the bitts by an experienced seaman, who should decide on what lowering hitch to use. There are several safe configurations that can be used, none of which will foul under any circumstances. To get it wrong could mean all the occupants being tipped out of the lifeboat and into the sea. It is a very important part of the lowering operation, as 'riding turns' or 'jamming hitches' would cause uncontrollable drops or jolts, placing a dangerous strain on the davits and tackles. In such a situation, the passengers in the boats being lowered would be terrified and in fear of their lives, sitting in cramped conditions and hanging high up over the icy waters of the North Atlantic. Another way to keep the weight down in the boat and off of the falls during lowering would be for those in charge to instruct the fitter men or crew to use the manropes or Jacob's ladders to enter the boat once it's in the water.

To maintain the trim of the lowering boats – in other words, to keep them level and ensure that one end doesn't go down quicker than the other – those in the boats should shout up to those on the boat deck. But communication simply by shouting up or down to each other would be difficult with the din of escaping steam forcing its way out of the funnel waste pipes. Coupled with this, the ship's lighting would have been poor in those days compared with the brilliant lights on ships today, and that, too, would have constituted a problem when working the boats that night. We should disregard the movies and touched-up pictures showing the whole scene lit up like a fairground. Quite clearly, lighting on the open decks that night would have been poor for an abandon-ship operation with so many passengers milling around.

It would also be the responsibility of those supervising to make sure that the drop zone directly underneath the lowered boats was clear of any floating debris or drifting craft. Once in the water, the correct procedure is to get away from the ship's side as soon as possible and to tether by painter, one boat to another. The priority for any lifeboat's coxswains is passenger safety. His boat should not remain alongside for too long, endangering the lives of its passengers. There is the danger of deck chairs and other wooden fitments being thrown over the side by those up on deck, hoping for some kind of lifesaver when they eventually end up in the water. Boats should group together for safety once away from the sinking vessel, allowing for the transferring of passengers, if necessary, and providing easy recognition for rescue vessels.

When temperatures are well above freezing, people in the water can hold on to grab lines around the gunwales of the lifeboat until they can be pulled inboard. Unfortunately, this was not an option on that night. Life expectancy in those icy waters would not have been more than five or six minutes. Clinker boats were the type used and it was that type of boat that was used on the *Titanic*. For all intents and purposes, those boats have always been of a good sturdy design. They are well tested over time and still in use today, although probably not as lifeboats. When I left the sea, lifeboats were usually carvel, diagonal, or of the moulded plastic type.

Many of the clinker boats on older ships in the early '50s were built by the methods that had been used for many years. They were of the same templates as those in the *Titanic's* day. This would have meant some kind of wood preservative, like a mixture of boiled oil and red lead; the planking would have overlapped and bedded in, one on top of the next. The planking or garboard strakes were secured at each end by mortise and tenon joints cut into the stem post and stern using a mixture of tallow and grease, horseshoe glue, or wedged pegs. In later years, copper nails and rivets became widely used.

The boats were usually powered by a set of oars, two spare oars, and a steering oar. If a boat had sails, sometimes it was just a main sail; other times, a mainsail and mizzen. When in dry conditions in the tropics, it wasn't unusual to drench the boats with a wash-down hose once in a while to prevent them from getting too dry and to keep the planking tight. Clinker boats were widely used in the Royal Navy. They were known as naval whalers or cutters and were sometimes screw-driven. Others were used as a sailing craft with a drop keel. It has been mentioned over the years that some of the *Titanic's* boats leaked on entering the water. Perhaps they were considered by some old sea dogs as being 'green' for not having been in the water for any length of time prior to use. This happened to Lifeboat 14, which leaked all night despite being bailed out continuously until being rescued the next morning.

A ship with thirty-two Welwyn davits, sixteen lifeboats, four collapsible boats, and a crew of around forty-five qualified seamen was not prepared to handle such an emergency. It would have been a seaman's nightmare. Despite the number of people who were saved, those of us who have served for many years in the industry are not surprised that so much went wrong that night. Despite the bad press the crew has had over the years, much of it from the inexperienced, I will always hold a certain admiration for what they managed to do in an almost impossible situation.

We should never forget that 75 per cent of the crew had drowned, and the other 25 per cent did what they could in helping to save the rest. Anyone with lengthy experience on passenger liners in the early '50s and '60s would probably be able to visualise the events that took place that night and would most likely agree with this write-up. To do this, of course, we would have to disregard what the movies have shown us over the years, although *A Night to Remember* was a movie that came close to depicting the actual events that took place that night.

AUTHOR'S SKETCH OF A TYPICAL WELWYN DAVIT CIRCA 1912

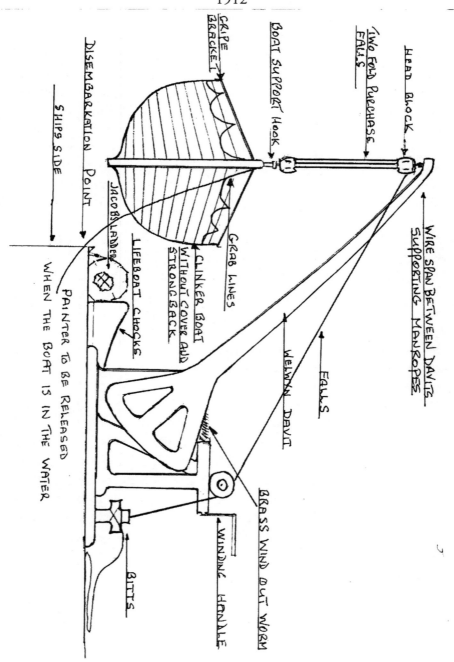

GRIPE BRACKET

BOAT SUPPORT HOOK

TWO FOLD PURCHASE FALLS

HEAD BLOCK

DISEMBARKATION POINT

SHIPS SIDE

JACOBS LADDER

LIFEBOAT CHOCKS

WITHOUT COVER AND STRONGBACK

CLINKER BOAT

GRAB LINES

WIRE SPAN BETWEEN DAVITS SUPPORTING MAN ROPES

WELWYN DAVIT

FALLS

PAINTER TO BE RELEASED WHEN THE BOAT IS IN THE WATER

BITTS

WINDING HANDLE

BRASS WIND OUT WORM

LOOKOUT PROCEDURES

On joining the Cunard White Star Line in the early 1950s, lookouts signed on the great 'Queen' liners as able seaman/lookouts and were paid extra for that duty. To my knowledge, no other shipping company paid extra for their lookouts. Perhaps this was also a direct result of the *Titanic* and the foul weather the North Atlantic could produce at any time of the year. Seamen going on lookout duty would go up to the crow's-nest by entering a door at the bottom of the mast in the deck department's quarters forward accommodation. Climbing up the ladder inside of the mast was not a job that would be readily welcomed by the claustrophobic or the overweight; there just wasn't a great deal of room in that tube. It was, however, considered to be pure luxury by seamen who previously would have had to climb a ladder on the outside of the mast to get into the crow's-nest. Climbing up and clinging to the foremast ladder in severe gales, rain, sleet, or snow, while wearing as much heavy gear as possible in order to keep warm once up there, was always going to be dangerous.

During my sea career, most shipping companies only posted lookouts from sunset to sunrise, but with Cunard White Star, lookouts were posted around the clock, and there was also a man on the docking bridge aft. There has been a great deal of comment about binoculars in the crow's-nest on the *Titanic*, but we never had such things when I stood lookout duty on the Queens or any other liners in those days. They were never considered necessary by maritime insurance. It was always the preference to scan the horizon with the naked eye. Maritime insurance always insisted that lookouts be posted despite any navigational aids on board, and in those days it wasn't uncommon for us to stand a lookout when navigating through the Suez or Panama canals.

During ice routine across the North Atlantic, lookouts were doubled up, but not in the crow's-nest as on board the *Titanic*. The extra lookout would stand his watch on the forecastle head, even though at times this wouldn't be much use in low-lying sea-fog situations. When such conditions occur, the lookout in the crow's-nest is very often in clear weather and sunshine but has difficulty making out the sea or the ship beneath him. When on lookout duty on the Queens in the English Channel and off of Southern Ireland, fishing boats were a problem. Very often in low-lying fog, only the tops of their masts could be visible. In those days, many fishing boats didn't have radar deflectors on their masts; as a result, they seldom showed up on the radar screens. Before the European fishing policy was adopted, there were many foreign fishing fleets in those waters, and there were quite a few 'missing' reports of these craft. Sometimes the Royal Navy got the blame for snagging fishing nets with submarines, although it was never proven. Those of us who worked as lookouts witnessed many a near miss with fishing boats.In my experience, lookouts on the *Titanic* would have had a tough call on the night of striking the iceberg, mainly because of the moonless night and the glass-like conditions of the sea. Difficulty in determining where the horizon meets the night sky is a phenomenon that very often gives lookouts a false impression of what is really out there.

In those regions, fog banks appear to come up from nowhere, and a ship can become shrouded in fog within minutes. With a bit of sea movement or wind and if the weather is clear, sometimes a slight wash becomes visible at the base of many icebergs. But depending on the size of the iceberg, a good sighting of several ship's lengths is required to avoid it when steaming at something like 22 knots. With low-level fog patches, and fog banks appearing as dark shapes with the stars still visible above them, it would have been difficult for a lookout to quickly determine what he was seeing. To make too many false snap decisions from the lookout is a bad practice that can annoy those on the bridge. It also shows some inexperience. With the speed of the vessel working against this type of decision-making, it's not hard to imagine how lookouts can sometimes feel.

It should also be considered that after two hours of standing in the crow's-nest in below-freezing temperatures, the lookout peering through the gloom at 22 knots would not be at his best. His concentration would suffer with the discomfort of the cold, and watering eyes would probably affect his vision. Having two men in a crow's-nest would restrict the movement needed to keep the circulation going. Some years later, the seamen's union managed to get ship owners to allow lookouts to work an hour up the mast in an open crow's-nest, but the discretion of the master was final. This meant that in bad weather conditions, a lookout could stand watch for an hour and then stand down for an hour before finishing his watch. In open crow's-nests, this would have been considered sensible and an obvious safety measure. Lookouts would be much more aware in foul weather conditions.

I hope the above rough guide will help some readers appreciate what seamen's duties were like at the time of *Titanic*, and what the crew was up against. Finally, I would like to add that the above write-up is an opinion based on my own experience. It is only a guide as to what might have taken place on *Titanic's* boat deck that night.

In writing and researching my mother's life story, my aim has been to write a refreshing narrative of her life and to record her story in the way she told it to her family throughout her life. It was to be a dedication to a wonderful, caring mother from one of her own children. It is her legacy, and one that we shall always remember her by. I've included her belief in the afterlife. As a family, we would laugh along with her on many issues, but that's how she told it, and that's how I've recorded it. I have gathered as much information as possible from my elder brothers and sisters. We have concluded that the narrative is accurate according to our memories, and we know she would have agreed with this account of her story.

In 1957, whilst I was serving on board Union Castle Line's *Cape Town Castle* in Cape Town, I had an interesting discussion with an Irish seaman from another ship in the port. He claimed his grandfather was a steerage passenger on the *Titanic* and was pulled out of the water into Lifeboat 14 as the ship was going down. On arriving home on leave a month later, I put this to my mother. She remembered someone being pulled out of the water muttering incoherently and her mother saying he sounded like an Irishman. It's extraordinary that the storyteller back in Cape Town chose Lifeboat 14 for his tale. It's also quite a coincidence, as the man never knew a thing about me.

Perhaps another coincidence worth a mention was my mother, at 99 years of age, being accompanied by my sister on a voyage of remembrance to the *Titanic* wreck site. They went in 1996 on a ship called the *Island Breeze*. Eighteen months later, the movie *Titanic* also showed a 100-year-old woman visiting the wreck site accompanied by her daughter.

EDITH HAISMAN CLOSE IN SOUTHAMPTON

Southampton City Council named the above road after our mother. The road is in the Freemantle area of Southampton and just a short walk from the house where Fred Fleet, the *Titanic's* lookout, used to live. Today I live just a five minutes' walk from Captain Rostron's gravesite. He was the master of the rescue ship *Carpathia*, and he took his ship, passengers, and crew through dangerous waters to rescue those on the *Titanic*. Without his professionalism and bravery, the death toll could have been much higher, and perhaps I might not be writing this today.

Contents

CHAPTER ONE

ICEBERG

Her father stood in the doorway of their cabin and said to them both, 'There's talk that the ship has struck an iceberg.' It was those fateful words that would mean that their lives were about to change forever. Edith and her mother, Elizabeth, were sharing a two-berth second-class cabin on board the *Titanic*. Her father, Thomas, was sharing a cabin further along the passageway with another gentleman.

It was almost midnight on Sunday, 14 April 1912, when Thomas Brown, still in evening dress, made this announcement to his wife and daughter. Just fifteen minutes earlier, both women had been woken up by what could be described as a shudder and several bumps. At that precise moment, Edith, occupying the upper berth, switched on her bunk light, parted the surrounding curtains, and peered down at her mother lying in the bunk below.

Elizabeth had also heard the noises and, on turning on her own bunk light, stared up at her daughter in total bewilderment. Edith quickly threw back her bed covers, swung her feet out, and climbed down the little varnished bunk ladder to the cabin floor. She crossed the cabin to the porthole and pulled the neat little curtains apart, opened the port glass, stuck her head out, and stared into the blackness. At first she could see nothing, but her eyes became accustomed to the darkness and she gradually began to make out the ship's lights reflecting on the water far below.

It was flat calm with no wind and, looking up, she could see a mass of stars in the moonless night sky. Looking down once more and toward the stern of the ship, she noticed a great deal of turbulence and foam as the ship's propellers churned up the water. The *Titanic* was going full astern. This was causing a great deal of vibration. Glasses clinked in the washstand, their door handle rattled, and the wood panelling and other fittings around their cabin creaked and squeaked.

Edith, somewhat mystified by what she was seeing and hearing, pulled her head back in order for her mother to see that the ship was stopping. Elizabeth crossed the cabin. With her head outside of the porthole, she quickly took in the scene before pulling her head back in. She again crossed the cabin to sit on the edge of her bunk. With a worried look on her face, she said to Edith, 'I wonder what that is all about, then?'

The forward part of the ship, where the deck crew, firemen, trimmers, and male emigrants had their accommodation, would have felt the impact with the iceberg more than anyone else on board. It wouldn't have taken most of them long to realise that something serious had just taken place. They would have turned out of their bunks to investigate the noises they had just heard. Some, later, had likened the initial impact to an anchor chain rubbing against the lower part of the ship's hull. Others had said that after the noise and bumps, it felt as though the ship had beached or run aground somewhere.

The more experienced seamen, familiar with this voyage across the North Atlantic, would begin to realise that the ship had collided with something extremely large. The heeling over directly on impact and the chunks of ice reported on the fore deck left them in no doubt that the ship had struck a huge iceberg. In the crow's-nest, the two lookouts had watched the iceberg pass on the starboard bow and felt the mast shudder as the vessel heeled over on striking the iceberg. Their feelings at that time were that it had been a close shave, and perhaps the vessel had veered off from a submerged ice shelf under the iceberg. They felt at that time that there was no cause for concern as the ship slowly came to a stop, and they waited until being dismissed some time later by the officer of the watch. On the bridge, Sixth Officer Moody had received the message from Fred Fleet in the crow's-nest and immediately passed it on to First Officer Murdoch. He instantly ordered the wheel to be put hard to port and double-rang all engine room telegraphs for the emergency 'full astern.' A ship of 46,000 tons travelling at over 21 knots would have responded to the wheel quite positively over a certain distance, but the *Titanic* had only swung some 22 degrees before striking the iceberg.

Captain Smith was called to the bridge immediately, and after going out on to the wing of the bridge, returned to the wheelhouse to assess the situation. Colliding with anything at the rate they were travelling would almost certainly mean that the vessel would be damaged somewhere. He immediately ordered the carpenter to sound all forward tanks and instructed the crew to inspect all forward compartments. At this point in time, Captain Smith would have waited until his ship had stopped and for damage reports to be brought up to the bridge. He would not have had any idea of any damage below the waterline or of the condition of the bottom plates. To move his ship in any direction without that information would be un-seamanlike and totally unnecessary at that time.

It's quite possible that after going astern for a certain period of time, the ship would have started making sternway. To counteract this Captain Smith would have ordered the engines to be put ahead briefly in an effort to stop the vessel dead in the water. The swirling water and turbulence around the ship's hull at that time would have made it difficult to determine whether the vessel was moving ahead or astern. Those on the bridge would have waited for the water to settle before carrying out that brief, ahead, engine movement.

Down in the engine room, immediately after the ringing of the telegraphs, there would have been a great deal going on as the boiler rooms would be ordered to shut dampers on fires and engineers began to wonder what was going to happen next. For the captain to give a double-ring astern in mid ocean without any previous standby notification from them was indeed an unfolding emergency situation. They had still not heard from the bridge what the problem was, although the lurching and bumps felt below meant they had struck something.

Up in the public rooms, some passengers were aware of a slight bump or two and a slight shudder, but in their part of the ship, the impact would have been the least noticeable. Some passengers playing cards and others at the bar enjoying a nightcap stopped briefly before they carried on with what they were doing. A few other passengers got up from their chairs and went out on to the promenade deck to meet others already out there, talking excitedly about an iceberg passing by so closely that it was almost possible to touch it! The ship's orchestra had almost finished playing for the night, but their leader, sensing some unease among the passengers, decided to carry on for a spell with a ragtime selection.

Passengers approached stewards on duty in the public rooms to enquire as to why the ship had stopped. Their replies were much the same, saying that they would soon be on their way again once they were clear of the surrounding ice field. There was also talk about how cold it had become. Several passengers were deciding to go to their cabins and turn in for the night. Some were advised to do this, as it was approaching midnight and most of the entertainment would be closing down for the night. There was little to see out on the open decks.

Down in their cabin on E Deck, Elizabeth was sitting on the edge of her bunk and showing some signs of concern about the latest developments. The excessive vibration felt earlier had now stopped, and the only sound was the faint whine of an electric motor somewhere far inside the ship. The night air from the open porthole made the cabin feel colder, and Elizabeth asked her daughter to close it to keep some warmth in the cabin. As Edith went again to the porthole, she took another look outside to see if anything else was happening. She found that the water was now quite still around the ship, and all was quiet.

On closing the porthole, Edith crossed the cabin to sit alongside her mother on the lower berth. She said, 'Everything seems so quiet.' Before her mother could answer, Thomas had tapped on their door and told them about the iceberg. He had advised them to put on warm clothing and life jackets and to follow him back up on deck. Elizabeth had looked at him in utter disbelief. Thomas, on the other hand, was not to be deterred. On entering the cabin, he reached up to the top of their wardrobe and pulled down the two life jackets stowed there. Elizabeth had always been quite a nervous person by nature, and this action by her husband wasn't helping matters at all. Edith, on the other hand, was 15 years of age. She wasn't worried at this stage and obediently did as she was told, knowing her father never made any rash decisions.

Both women proceeded to put on warm jumpers and topcoats before Thomas began to help them on with their life jackets. Elizabeth remained speechless as her husband busied himself about her, adjusting the bulky life jacket and tying the tapes in front with a large bow. The life jackets were made up of cumbersome, square chunks of cork held together with stitched duck canvass. When placed over the head, they hung from the shoulders and tied at the waist. With their heavy clothing on, both women looked twice their size. This caused Edith to forget the seriousness of the situation and giggle for a moment.

Before leaving their cabin, Edith spotted her diary on her bunk. As she never went anywhere without it, she quickly put it in her pocket as they went out. She had left behind a beautiful gold-and-coral necklace her father had bought for her in London, but at this point in time, her diary was all that mattered. As they walked along the plush, carpeted passageway toward the first flight of stairs, Elizabeth wanted to know why her husband wasn't wearing his life jacket. His reply was that they shouldn't worry too much about that at the moment; he would find one later. The important thing was to get them up to the boat deck.

EDITH'S DIARY, WHICH SHE TOOK WITH HER INTO LIFEBOAT 14

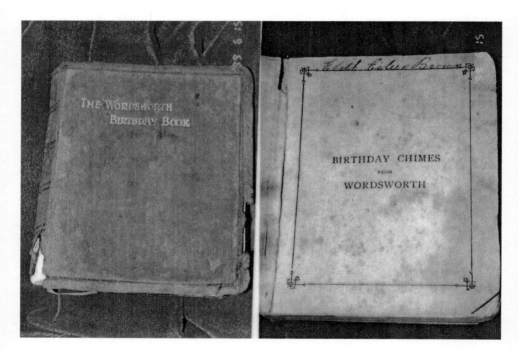

As they made their way up the first flight of stairs, Edith thought the stairs seemed easier to climb and not quite so steep as the last time she climbed them. The *Titanic* was settling down at the head, but Edith was not to realise that at the time. They continued up more flights of stairs with their carved banisters, passing beautiful wood panelling on both sides as they made their way up to the boat deck. As they went, they passed many passengers on their way down, muttering and claiming it was too cold to remain up there for long. Many of those passengers were in evening dress, and some were wearing coats over night attire. Several of them were wearing life jackets. In the passageways, stewards could be seen rapping on doors and calling out, 'Everyone up with life jackets on, please!' There was little response. The whole scene was quite relaxed; with the odd quip from some about having a good night's sleep disturbed. Others just closed their doors again after the steward's call.

On arrival at the final flight of stairs, they stepped out on to the boat deck and into the icy cold night air, joining a group of people already gathering around Lifeboat 14. While in their cabin, Thomas had seen a small notice behind the door saying that passengers from that cabin should assemble at lifeboat station fourteen during any emergency. Below their position on the boat deck, they could hear lively music coming up from the decks below. Elizabeth nervously said to her husband that some people didn't seem too worried about the situation; perhaps things weren't as bad as they were being made out to be. Thomas's firm reply left her in no doubt that as far as he was concerned; they were doing the right thing. It was better to be prepared in case things did get out of hand and they had to get into those boats. People remained in small groups around Lifeboat 14, indulging in light-hearted conversation as they watched seamen take the covers off of the boats and prepare them for lowering into the water.

Edith was feeling tired after being woken from a deep sleep. She was thinking about how good it would be if the whole thing was called off and she could get back into her comfortable bunk. With puffs of vapour from her breath visible as she spoke, Edith asked her father how long he thought this exercise was going to last. He told her to be patient; he would be tucking them both in for the night once the emergency had been called off. However, Thomas wasn't too convinced by his own reassurance. And he knew he would have to calm Elizabeth, who was becoming increasingly unhappy at the way things were looking.

There was considerable talk about ice on the fore deck, and some of the men at the third-class end of the ship were seen throwing chunks of it around. This was another alarming development. If ice had fallen from an iceberg to the fore deck, the iceberg must have been huge enough to tower over the ship's bow and forward decks at the time of the collision. There was also mention that some of the third-class passengers in the forward section of the ship were leaving their accommodation and the well deck area, carrying suitcases and bundles of their belongings. Up to this point, there had been no official indication that anything was wrong other than stewards directing passengers to go up on deck with their life jackets on. There had been no alarm bells or blasts from the ship's whistle to indicate that an emergency was in fact taking place. This could have been a deliberate decision to prevent panic.

Captain Smith would have known soon after the collision that his ship was in a precarious situation. He would have been able to tell by the trim, an inclination that soon becomes evident to a professional seafarer. He would also have realised that there just wasn't enough lifesaving gear on the ship for everyone and that a great loss of life was imminent if the worst was to happen. It was not going to help matters to let that be known. Too much information given out to passengers would have, in all probability, created a far greater loss of life from panic. There was much chatter amongst the passengers, and wild speculation as to what had actually happened. There was talk that an abandon-ship procedure would be carried out until vital repairs had been done, just as a safety precaution. Others were saying that the ship had been damaged and would later get under way again at a reduced speed. There were also several mutterings and a claim that there wasn't anything to worry about, as the ship was deemed unsinkable. However, passengers and crew alike were behaving in an orderly fashion, although the looks on some faces revealed that there were those who didn't appear to be convinced by what they were overhearing.

On the bridge, Captain Smith had received word from the carpenter that a hatch cover in the forepeak had been forced off as water rushed into that section. Air could be heard hissing out of the fore peak air vents. This was an indication that the ship was flooding in those compartments. Later reports revealed that accommodation and

8

storerooms in the lower decks of the forward section were also flooding. Captain Smith was soon to learn that water was finding its way into the mailrooms, and mail sorters were in the process of taking sacks of mail up to higher levels. Other reports coming up to the bridge were the most serious so far. Boiler room six was also flooding, although watertight doors had been shut. This meant that the ship might be damaged right through her first five compartments. That being the case, it would only be a matter of time before the ship foundered.

Captain Smith had ordered a junior officer to get Mr Andrews, the ship's designer, on the bridge as soon as possible. He didn't have far to go, as the chief designer had already arrived in the wheelhouse and bumped into the junior officer on entering the chart room. Clutching several rolls of blueprints, he laid them out on the chart room table, revealing *Titanic's* innermost construction details. Thomas Andrews had been awake at the time of the collision with the iceberg. He knew by the way the ship had shuddered that she just had to be damaged somewhere. In the chart room beneath the glow of a soft orange light, Captain Smith and Thomas Andrews leant forward and began to scrutinise the ship's forward compartments and the adjacent storerooms and cofferdams. From the reports coming up to the bridge, it became clear that the ship was taking in water from the first five compartments and adjacent areas. This meant that there was a fracture or fractures below the waterline of some 300 feet, which left both men fearing the worst. When asked by the commander what it all meant, Thomas Andrews, with an ashen look on his face, replied in a choked voice that the *Titanic* could stay afloat with four compartments flooded, but not five. He went on to say that the bulkhead between the fifth and sixth compartments only went as high as E Deck. Once the water rose to that level, it would overflow into the next compartment and so on throughout the ship.

Both men looked at each other in the stark realisation that, just four and half days into her maiden voyage, the *Titanic* was doomed. Captain Smith then asked Thomas Andrews how long he thought she could stay afloat. The ship's designer looked up at the chart room clock and then down at his blueprints. He pencilled calculations before he finally declared that they could remain afloat for two hours at the most. There was no doubt that the vessel was seriously damaged below the waterline and probably along the bottom plates, although this damage would always be speculated upon but never fully known.

9

Just forty-five minutes after the collision with the iceberg, it was estimated by the trim of the vessel that she had have taken on at least 10,000 tons of water in her forward compartments. At this point, Captain Smith ordered all his officers on to the bridge for a briefing. He declared that the situation was grave; the ship was going to founder, and an abandon-ship procedure was to be acted upon immediately. Pistols were handed out to the deck officers who thought they might need them, with orders only to use them if panic broke out or if all other forms of persuasion had been exhausted. All boats were to be immediately cleared away, and it would be women and children first. This would have been normal procedure in such a situation, and there's no doubt that this discipline was adhered to in most cases.

The ship's orchestra had moved up to the boat deck as more and more people were finding their way there, and they continued to play popular tunes from that era. Seamen continued to clear away boats for lowering. The incline toward the bow was becoming more pronounced as time went by. The night appeared to be very still. The sounds of regular hissing came from the funnel waste pipes, and the sounds of men's voices could be heard now and then around the boats as they worked on them. There was the squeaking from tackles and the odd bumps in the boats as crew arranged oars and gear before the boats were raised from their chocks in readiness for swinging out. Several passengers were returning to their cabins to put on extra clothing, and some even decided it was time to go down to turn in for the night.

This was not to last, however. Ship's stewards, stewardesses, and all other personnel were given strict orders that all cabins were to be vacated immediately and all passengers told to proceed to the boat deck with life jackets on. Up to this time, the crewmembers were performing their duties in an orderly, professional manner, although it was becoming abundantly clear that they could have done with more professional seamen to assist them. The crew treated all classes firmly but politely, assisting all women and children into the boats and trying to remain light-hearted and cheerful.

At this time, Elizabeth was becoming increasingly distressed as she saw more boats being lowered and people being ordered into them with greater urgency. Thomas was doing his best to calm her down by saying that she shouldn't upset herself, as he would be looking for another boat once he knew they were settled in Lifeboat 14 and away from the ship. He knew she didn't believe him, but what more could he say at a time like this? Edith held tightly on to one of her father's arms with both of hers as she stood alongside of him, stamping first one foot and then the other in order to maintain some circulation in her feet.

Their lifeboat had Fifth Officer Lowe in command. He was a Welshman in his late twenties with a reputation as a bit of a disciplinarian, and he was in the process of ordering people into the boat in no uncertain terms. His voice had authority and could be heard on several occasions shouting at some of the crew to, 'Get a bloody move on!' In the first-class public rooms, the emergency was still being treated as more of an inconvenience, rather than the disaster it was quickly becoming. Passengers were still finishing off their drinks and card games. Others were sitting around in life jackets, appearing to wait for the whole thing to be called off so that they could get on with what they had been doing. Many had assembled in the gymnasium and were being advised by the instructor to use some of the equipment in order to take their minds off of events and to keep themselves warm. Out on the boat deck, more and more passengers were arriving from the lower decks. Elizabeth wondered how so many people were expected to get into so few lifeboats. Thomas tried to reassure her that it was quite amazing just how many people could be accommodated in the lifeboats. Unconvincingly, he said that once seated, there shouldn't be any problem.

As people were being helped into the boats, there was a sudden ear-shattering roar. The safety valves had lifted, causing steam to be blasted out of the waste pipes at the top of the funnels. This build-up of pressure was the result of the ship having a good head of steam before the collision. Now that she had stopped, that pressure had to be vented off to prevent her boilers from exploding. The continuous deafening roar only made matters worse. All communication between officers, crew, and passengers had to be carried out by shouting through cupped hands. People were beginning to show real fear, as many thought the ship would explode beneath them. They couldn't understand why the steam was being blasted off with such force.

Women carrying small children made attempts to cover the children's ears with their hands or shawls. Other families clung to each other, fearing the worse. The poor lighting on ships in those days increased the problems the crew faced, and with the din from the escaping steam, the lowering of lifeboats and the giving out of orders was becoming a problem. After some twenty minutes or so, the orchestra could be heard playing lively music once again as the roar of steam slowly abated. The musicians were doing a superb job and showing great dedication to duty, and their efforts were having a calming effect on many of the frightened passengers. The preparation and lowering of lifeboats with Welwyn davits meant that the boat's crew needed plenty of room to prepare the boats and passengers needed to be kept clear.

Up in the radio shack, both operators were having one of their busiest days of the voyage, going through a heavy workload, transmitting passengers' messages through the wonderful medium of radio. The senior operator, Jack Phillips, had relieved Harold Bride earlier in the day and continued with the never-ending demand for the transmitting of passengers' messages, as they were in range of Cape Race. Many messages were of a trivial nature and were sent merely to impress friends and relatives in America and to show the wonders of ship-to-shore radio. Both operators had become quite irritable from long sessions working the equipment and the incessant pips in their ears from the Morse code signals.

During the day, they had interruptions from other ship's operators breaking into their transmissions with ice reports and, due to their huge workload, some of those reports remained on their desk and not on the bridge. Harold Bride had arrived up in the radio shack just around midnight to relieve Phillips from his duties when Captain Smith entered the radio room and ordered that they send for assistance. The radio operator was not quite sure how serious the situation was and wanted to know if a distress call should be sent out. 'Yes!' replied the captain. 'Right away!' Phillips immediately set about sending the signal of CQD, recognised at that time as the international distress call. As Captain Smith stood behind him, waiting to see if there was any quick response, Phillips turned to his commander and said, 'Shall I try the new distress signal of SOS, sir?'

'Yes!' replied the captain. 'Use them both.'

The response to their distress call was almost immediate. Within minutes they had received several replies from ships within their range, the first from the German steamer *Frankfurt* at approximately 12. 20 a.m., but they gave no position. Others included a Russian tramp steamer and the CPR liner *Mount Temple*. There was another reply from the liner *Virginian*. All of these ships had acknowledged the distress call, but their distance from the *Titanic* was a major factor. The steamer closest to the *Titanic* was Cunard Line's *Carpathia*, steaming in the opposite direction out of New York with 700 passengers on board, bound for a Mediterranean cruise.

Harry Cotham, the *Carpathia's* radio operator, on picking up the *Titanic's* distress call, at first thought it was a mistake. He knew that he had better confirm the message before calling the captain; if he had got it wrong, he would feel a bit stupid and never live it down. He contacted the *Titanic* for confirmation of the message he had just received. He wanted to know if there was any difficulty and if any assistance was required. Almost immediately, the Morse code quickly answered Cotham's signal, confirming that there was no doubt about the distress call. The *Titanic* was sinking, and they should proceed as fast as possible to the position given by Jack Phillips. A great loss of life was imminent.

Harry Cotham awakened Captain Rostron, and there was a moment of disbelief as he waited for it to sink in. Suddenly and without further ado, Captain Rostron threw his heavy bridge coat on over his pyjamas and rushed up to the bridge. On entering the wheelhouse, he ordered the helmsman to alter course 180 degrees. Then, going into the chart room, he leant over the chart table and began to work out the distance from the stricken liner. After a few pencil calculations and moving his slide rule about the chart, he notified the engine room of the situation. He told the engineers to, 'Give her all she had.'

They would be racing into dangerous waters for that time of the year, as there was much ice about. Captain Rostron also had the safety of his own crew and passengers to think about as he set a course for *Titanic's* last reported position. The lookouts were doubled up, and the *Carpathia's* usual cruising speed of 14 knots had been increased to between 16 and 17 knots, which was just about all she could handle.

High up on *Titanic's* boat deck, Edith, pointing to the horizon, said excitedly, 'Look, father! There's a light over there. Perhaps they will come over to help us.'

Thomas and Elizabeth both looked in the direction of their daughter's pointing finger and could also make out a light flickering on the horizon.

'I do believe you're right my dear,' Thomas said. 'Let's hope so.'

Several other passengers had their attention drawn to the light flickering on the horizon that night, but it has always been a mystery as to why that vessel never responded to rockets, distress calls, or Morse lamp signals.

The Leyland freighter *Californian* had stopped in the same ice field as *Titanic*, as her previous reports had indicated, leaving an apprenticed ship's officer on the bridge. It would have been quite normal in those days for that to be the case when stopped in ice, and on larger vessels it might well have been just a junior officer on the bridge. It has been established from reports that he had seen what appeared to be a large liner on the horizon signalling with a Morse lamp, but, as his own Morse lamp was giving him trouble, he failed to reply. It was during that same period that a 'donkey man' (engineroom artificer) from the *Californian's* engine room decided to go up on deck for a smoke, and he claimed that he had seen rockets being sent up from the *Titanic*.

On the *Titanic's* boat deck, there was now a greater urgency to get women and children into the boats, as ever-increasing numbers were appearing on the boat deck from their cabins below. Down in the forward compartments, where cargo holds and baggage rooms were situated, there was extensive flooding. Water was creeping up the spiral staircase to the firemen's quarters. The lamp trimmer, who had been woken earlier by the impact of the iceberg, was now going along the passageways banging on all the doors of watch-keepers and shouting, 'Everybody up! She's flooded out!'

Doors began to open, and sleepy-eyed men peered out, wondering what all the commotion was about. Many were only clad in underpants or long johns. Some were stark naked as they looked up and down the passageways from behind half-closed doors. They were soon to learn that things were indeed looking bad. Water had reached the top of the spiral staircase and was now creeping along to their cabins, bringing with it bits and pieces of debris from the decks below. Seeing this for the first time, the men grabbed what gear they could and, splashing through icy, ankle-deep water, made for the stairway leading to the upper decks.

By this time, the deck crew was up and attending to the boats. It would soon become clear that there just weren't enough professional seamen to do what was going to be expected of them in the next hour or so.

In boiler room six, water had gushed in from the starboard side, taking with it chunks of coal from the bunkers, and splashing black, oily slurry about the boiler room. The firemen and trimmers working the boilers were stripped to the waist, and they were splattered with this filthy, ice-cold black stream of slurry, along with bits of coal and debris. The full shock of this ice-cold torrent would have left them breathless as they thrashed about in the water after being knocked over by the sheer force of it gushing into the boiler room.

As the boiler room continued to flood, huge clouds of steam erupted as the water came into contact with hot boiler casings. The water, knee-high and rising fast, meant only one thing to the engineer in charge, and that was to get the men out of there as quickly as possible. 'Everyone out and up to the boat deck!' he shouted. It was hard for him to be heard above the din of hissing steam and the cries from some of the men, but they knew by his waving and pointing topside exactly what he meant.

Scrambling one after the other up the vertical iron ladders, coughing and spluttering, they made their way up to the decks above. The engineers knew they would have to stay below for as long as possible, working the pumps and generally trying to keep on top of the situation as it was developing. The way the water was rising gave great cause for alarm, although it was hoped that the closed watertight doors would keep back most of the flow for the time being. The main concern was to keep the generators running to keep the pumps and lights working for as long as possible. The positive displacement pumps would need to be going at their full capacity and, although very effective under what could be described as normal situations, it was becoming clear that they would never keep up with this torrent flooding the boiler rooms.

Cold water was being fed into the boilers to counteract the build-up of pressure, and this would have been a normal procedure under such circumstances.

All watertight doors from the bridge had been closed immediately after striking the iceberg, but they could be operated manually. The chief engineer would have decided that they should be opened to inspect other parts of the engine and boiler rooms. He ordered two firemen to open the watertight doors to boiler room five. These men then went about cranking open the doors of boiler rooms one through four, finally reaching boiler room five. It was here that they heard tremendous rumblings and great popping noises from behind the bulkhead separating the two boiler rooms. The trimmers and firemen were working frantically to draw fires in their attempts to minimise the danger from explosion. They remained in the stifling heat and the din of escaping steam, hoping that in some way their efforts would save the ship.

It was well after one in the morning when the chief engineer ordered one of his junior engineers topside to gain first-hand knowledge of how the emergency was developing. He knew how busy the ship's deck officers would be at such a time, and getting a first-hand report from one of his own engineers would give him a better picture of the way things were looking. From below, he knew the ship was turning increasingly down at the head and also showing signs of listing to port, but it would be helpful to know the position at the present time on the open decks. He had reports from the tunnels (propeller shaft corridors) that told him in no uncertain terms that the bilges were draining toward the forward sections and strum boxes (pumping-out drain covers) were becoming exposed.

At the stern of the ship, passengers were having a quieter time of it compared to their counterparts at the forward end of the vessel. The third-class cabins at the stern would normally experience some vibration from the vessel's triple screws when running at cruising speed. After experiencing the ship going full astern just an hour ago, they may well have realised from the greatly increased vibration that something was wrong. The talk of chunks of ice on the fore deck hadn't appeared to trouble those passengers at the after end, many not realising the ice's significance. More and more third-class passengers were coming up from the working alleyway, known as the Scotland road, to join some friends and relatives on the after well deck. The working alleyway ran the whole length of the ship and was used by the crew for services throughout the ship. Other than passing through second- and first-class accommodation, this was the only route the third-class passengers could take to link up with those at the other end.

It has been reported that many who went through the accommodation in trying to find their way to the boat deck had lost their sense of direction and ended up back where they started from. It has also been reported that stewards were sending third-class passengers back to their accommodation until ordered to proceed to the boat deck. The class system in those days was such that many people in third class didn't expect to be considered until the other two classes had been looked after. These people resigned themselves to waiting it out. Some stewards had been ordered to deal with the third class, but to keep control of the situation at all times for fear of things getting out of hand.

'Women and children first! The rest of you stand well back away from the boat!' was the cry from Fifth Officer Lowe as the crew began to assist passengers into Lifeboat 14.

The growing throng of people coming up to the boat deck was causing considerable concern to the officer in charge. It was becoming apparent that there just wasn't enough room in the boat to accommodate all of them. There was some shouting between passengers. A few children were beginning to cry. The crew shouted above them all, trying maintain some control. It would be dangerous around the boat, as the falls (the ropes lowering the boat) and some running gear would have been lying on deck in readiness for lowering. Passengers standing too close to the work would not only be a hindrance; with the poor lighting on the boat deck, they could easily foul up the lines as the crew organised the running gear to lower the boats.

With the boat swung out, two seamen should have been at either end for the lowering of the falls around the bitts. Another should have served as back-up. This would have been vital to ensure ropes ran free, preventing riding turns or crippled lines from fouling the smooth lowering process with a boat load of passengers. Qualified seaman would have known that if any of those problems had arisen, the falls could jam, causing riding turns, long drops, or jolts. The trim of the boat could also be seriously compromised.

Elizabeth had stopped crying, but Thomas continued to hold her close. He had his arm around her waist as they watched the boats being cleared away along the boat deck. Edith was watching the women and children being helped by their men folk as they stepped across into Lifeboat 12, awkwardly standing on the cross benches before sitting down.

She was trying her best to remain calm, but her mother's present state wasn't helping matters much. She, too, was dreading the moment when they would have to get into their boat and leave her father behind.

At this time, their newfound friends and dining companions, Rev. Carter and his wife, Lillian, had joined them on the boat deck. Lifeboat 7 was one of the first away, but it was only half full. The first officer instructed the boat to return alongside to pick up other passengers from other boats or from the sea. Lifeboat 5 was soon in the water, with Third Officer Pitman in overall charge of both boats. These were tethered bow-to-stern with a line, which was the correct procedure. Other boats were in the process of being lowered, some swinging about clumsily as the boat's crew tried to steady them by pushing their oars against the ship's side.

There were shouts from the boats being lowered to loved ones left back on deck. Others in the boats were crying loudly and sobbing at the realisation that the once-mighty liner was now doomed. The crews were shouting to the passengers in the boats to sit down and keep still. It was a precarious situation, for many boats still hung from their davits. There was a dog barking somewhere up by the funnel deck, a continuous hissing from the waste pipes at the top of the funnels, and the strains of lively music still being heard over the ship's many noises. The foremost funnel had become silent, probably due to the forward boiler rooms becoming totally flooded.

On the great North Atlantic liners, lookouts were posted on the docking bridge aft, a small, raised deck running from one side to the other at the stern of the ship. It was here that the emergency steering gear was situated. There was a ship's wheel and a magnetic compass, usually under a duck canvas cover or some other protection. A quartermaster would stand a short watch on the docking bridge, and it was here that he witnessed a huge iceberg passing close by as the ship was going at full astern. After the engines had stopped, he was ordered from the bridge to take distress rockets up to the wheelhouse immediately.

Up in the first-class staterooms and cabins, the rich and famous were being helped on with their life jackets by their own personal manservant's or maids. They were being advised on what to wear and what little comforts they could take along with them. They had first-class stewards to escort them to their lifeboats and stewardesses to help their wives and children. There were some first-class passengers who showed extraordinary courage, like Benjamin Guggenheim and Mr And Mrs Strauss, who chose to stay behind and give their places in the lifeboats to others.

As the boats continued to be lowered, manropes could be seen hanging limply from the davit head wire spans, and Jacob's ladders were seen hanging down the ship's side to the water. The lighting was poor, and the din around them made it difficult for the crews in the boat to be heard when shouting instructions up to those lowering the boats. These factors could have caused serious mishaps in the boats, as those on deck would have had no indication of the trim of the boat. Some boats were reported to have landed heavily in the water; others hit one end before the other.

Lifeboat 14 went down the ship's side in jolts and jerks before finally hitting the water, causing many to fall about the boat. As a result, the boat shipped a great deal of water. According to Edith years later, it was ankle-deep, and, despite bailing, it remained in the bottom of the boat throughout the night.

Stewardesses were doing a good job helping women and children to the boats from all classes. They returned below to repeat the operation until they were sure everyone was out of their cabins. There were also many bellboys standing in a group on the boat deck. They were smoking, laughing, and chatting among themselves, not really grasping the situation for what it was. Most were no older than fourteen or fifteen, and they had no idea what they were expected to do, other than to keep out of the way. They were neither men nor boys, but they were crew, and their chances of getting into a lifeboat that night were extremely remote. Like the other men on board, they would have to take their chances once all the lifeboats had gone.

As the passengers continued to be loaded into the boats, there was the occasional swishing sound of a rocket streaking into the night sky, lighting up everyone's faces as it burst into a shower of sparks above them. Captain Smith had apparently walked from one wing of the bridge to the other, observing the way the forward part of his ship was gradually sinking lower. The water was beginning to pour on to the forecastle head. This was coming up from the spurling pipes (cable locker pipes), confirming that the cable lockers were completely flooded. As the water began to wash over the deck gunwales, the captain looked aft at the crowded boat deck. Passengers were clambering into the remaining boats, still hanging from their davits at deck level in readiness for lowering. Turning away with a feeling of utter despair, he walked back along the sloping deck and entered the wheelhouse. Glancing up to the clock, he noticed the time. It was 1.20 a.m. He thought briefly that just one hour and forty minutes ago, the *Titanic* had been steaming through the night, the pride of the British merchant fleet. Now she was mortally damaged and dying in a lethally cold sea. From what he had just seen, she would take many with her when she took her final plunge.

Letting his glance fall to a small blackboard situated beneath the clock, he read the last details written in chalk by a quartermaster at the change of the last watch. It read, 'Air temperature 32 degrees. Sea temperature 31 degrees.'

Written beneath that were the engine revolutions on the outboard port and starboard engines and the central screw revolutions. Captain Smith had altered course earlier in the day, taking the ship on a track some sixteen nautical miles further south than the reported ice field. His might have wished he had maintained his original course and put the engine room on standby; perhaps the outcome would have been much different. Leaving Southampton late, and then having to stop to avoid an incident off of Dock Head, meant that his ship had not made up that extra time. She was in different position than she would have been if she had sailed on time.

Fate had dealt him a lethal blow; there was no doubt about that. The negligence of the Board of Trade in allowing the ship to go to sea with insufficient lifeboats might also have passed through his mind at some time. And he may have questioned not having his ship on standby whilst on ice routine. This would have enabled the engine room to have engineers on standby at the throttles. The revs would have been slightly reduced, with the valves and bypass systems ready to be acted on effectively, allowing precious time before the collision. This would have been the normal procedure during ice routine. Although the *Titanic* may well have collided with the iceberg regardless, the impact might have been far less with these systems in operation. He would have known that the instant avoidance of a collision at Dock Head on leaving Southampton was a direct result of the ship's engine room being on standby. It was proof of how quickly engine room movements can be acted upon with engineers on standby.

Turning back to look out of the wheelhouse windows, he could see the disappearing jib of the cable locker derrick on the forecastle head. He knew it wouldn't be long before he would be joining others, perhaps hundreds of them, in those icy waters.

High up on the boat deck, the ship's orchestra continued to play light-hearted music as boats were lowered to the water and pulled away from the stricken liner. On the wing of the bridge, Captain Smith shouted, using a loud hailer, ordering boats that weren't full to return to the ship and pick up survivors.

Rev. Carter took his wife to Lifeboat 12. After a short time, he returned to assist Thomas with Edith and Elizabeth.

The time the Browns were all dreading had finally arrived. Edith and her mother were helped into Lifeboat 14.

THOMAS AND ELIZABETH

CHAPTER TWO

CAPE TOWN

Thomas William Solomon Brown had been born in Blackheath, London, in 1853. He was a widower, and he had two sons and two daughters from a previous marriage. Although Edith knew little of her father's background, she knew he'd had a brother who had been a ship's captain, and that he had drowned at sea. Thomas owned the Masonic Hotel in Worcester, Cape Province. Later, he also owned the Mountain View Hotel in Cape Town. He had shares in wine and brandy companies and many interests in cottage properties in False Bay and Muizenberg. He was a well-respected businessman, well liked in the community, and a prominent Freemason. He was a short man of medium build with almost white hair and a bushy moustache to match. He had a round, kindly face and a pleasant disposition. He was always smartly dressed.

Edith's mother was born Elizabeth Catherine Ford. She was twenty years younger than Thomas. She was related to a wealthy Afrikaans family by the name of Louwe who owned farms and dairies around Durban and the Durban Ville areas. Elizabeth was of medium build and height and could be described as having a matronly and Victorian look about her. Despite that, she was an extremely loving and devoted to those close to her. Since marrying Thomas, she had wanted for nothing. She made it a rule never to interfere in any of his business affairs.

Edith was born at the Masonic Hotel in Worcester on 27 October 1896. She was a small child with slender limbs who could have been described as being slightly underweight, but she remained strong and healthy despite that. She was the first child of this marriage. She was followed by a sister, born four years later at the Masonic Hotel, who tragically died at the age of eight from diphtheria at the Mountain View Hotel in Cape Town. Edith was devoted to her parents, and her whole upbringing was focused toward her one day becoming a young lady. She was receiving a convent education and was learning to play the piano. Young girls in those days stayed close to their parents. As a result, she had always been a great help to her mother and father around the hotel.

Elizabeth had always kept in close contact with her sister, whose husband worked for the National Bank of Seattle. Throughout 1910–11, her sister Josephine had sent letters full of praise at the way life in America was booming. She had suggested many times that they should think about moving there and starting up their own hotel business. Over several months, Thomas and Elizabeth had many discussions about the prospects of starting a new business venture in a foreign country. Elizabeth was becoming more convinced, as time went by, that it would be a good move for all of them. Thomas, on the other hand, was a bit more reluctant, possibly due to the fact that he was approaching 60. He knew that his wife was not one to try to interfere and force the issue. However, he was fully aware of how excited his wife was at the prospect of a new life in Seattle. Reflecting on the quiet life his wife and daughter were living in Cape Town, he thought that it was perhaps the right thing to do after all. Shortly after Christmas of 1911, on a beautiful morning in Cape Town, Thomas, dressed in topper and tails and swinging his silver-topped walking cane, strode down Adderley Street toward the Union Castle Line shipping offices. He had worked out that if he could arrange a passage to England within the following couple of months, he stood a good chance of booking a passage on the great new liner that everyone was talking about. He had read in the *Cape Town Argus* that the *Titanic* would be sailing from Southampton on 10 April 1912 on her maiden voyage to New York. He realized that they would have to sail on the *Saxon* in February to give them some time in London for sightseeing. It would also be an opportune time for all of them to shop in the wonderful stores in Oxford Street and Bond Street before the next stage of their journey to America.

Before entering the shipping office, Thomas looked along Adderley Street and up at Table Mountain, which always looked quite spectacular in the early morning sunshine. The top of the mountain was draped in cloud cover, known as the 'table cloth,' and at one end, Lion's Head could be seen poking through a ring of cloud at its very top. He pondered for a moment at the decision he was about to make, but he realised they had given it a lot of thought. Business was slow in the Cape after the Boer War, and with that in mind, he entered the shipping offices without further ado.

As he did so, he felt very faint and was forced to sit on a chair just inside the entrance. A young clerk came over to him and asked in a clipped South African accent if he was feeling all right. 'Yes,' replied Thomas as he wiped his brow with his handkerchief. The clerk asked if he would like a glass of water. Thomas thanked him and took a long drink before handing the almost empty glass back to him. This was a strange feeling. It was, as he said later, a combination of panic and fear, but why? Once his colour returned, he went on and purchased the tickets for their planned voyage to England.

On stepping back outside into the bright sunshine, he began to slowly walk back up Adderley Street, still trying to understand what may have come over him a short while ago. He stopped a bit further along the street and again looked up at the mountain with its slate grey rock faces, scattered light and dark green foliage, and splashes of purple. Taking in this natural splendour, he had a feeling that he would miss this place once away from it for any length of time. He began to walk faster, this time realising that if things didn't work out abroad, they could always come back. He would make provision for such an event by leaving some of his stocks and shares in South Africa to mature. He then entered his hotel and immediately saw Edith and Elizabeth arranging flowers in the foyer. He went over to tell them the good news. As he approached them, they looked away from what they were doing and, turning toward him as he approached, noticed the excitement on his face.

Thomas, with arms outstretched as though to embrace them both, declared, 'It's done! We sail for England in February.'

That afternoon after all the excitement, Edith was sitting upstairs, looking out of one of the windows of their private apartments at the street below. There was a penny whistle band passing below, beating drums and dancing as they went. They were always fun to watch with their lively music and carnival atmosphere, and Edith quite enjoyed watching the spectacle passing below her vantage point. Her mother entered the room and stood behind her, and they both observed the entertainment going on below the window. Elizabeth asked her daughter if she thought she might miss Cape Town once they had left for America. Edith said she didn't really know, but she was looking forward to the voyage on the great new ship that everyone was talking about. Turning away from the scene beneath them, she looked at her mother and said, 'Do you think Father really wants to go?'

Elizabeth, looking at her daughter with a reassuring smile on her face, replied, 'I'm sure he does, my dear. Your father would never do anything that he hasn't thought about first. That's why he has always been very successful in everything he does.' Finally, she said, 'If it's as good as they say it is in America, then we've nothing to lose and everything to gain.' With that, both women continued to look out of the window at the carnival below.

Thomas had been busy the past few weeks, arranging all his finances, especially those holdings in the various wine and brandy companies. He had been a shrewd businessman, taking care to leave behind the shares and holdings that would increase in value and were considered to be safe. They may well come in handy, he thought, if things didn't work out too well in Seattle and they needed something to fall back on. With his many respected friends in financial circles, he had little trouble in finding buyers for some of his assets, and the sale at £14,000 was considered a good price for the hotel. He was also pleased with the sale of his toyshop on Adderley Street, which was destined to become a barbershop.

One evening before departure, Thomas was having a drink in the bar of his hotel with an old business acquaintance of his. Their conversation went something like this:

'I've known you for many years, Tom, and I've never known you to make any rash decisions. To sell up everything at your age and to embark on a new life and business venture in another country must have left you many sleepless nights.' After packing tobacco into the bowl of his pipe and appearing thoughtful, he went on. 'It's a courageous thing to do, Tom; I'll grant you that. But aren't you comfortable enough here without going through all those uncertainties of setting yourself up again?'

Thomas swirled his brandy around in the bottom of his glass thoughtfully, gently puffing on his cigar before answering. 'George, I could have stayed here in the Cape for the rest of my days and remained reasonably contented, but things are slow here at the moment, and I want to give my wife and daughter a better chance in life before I get much older.' He added with a chuckle, 'besides, there's plenty of steam left in the old fellow yet. No doubt you'll be reading about me in the *Cape Town Argus* when I've made my fortune.'

With that, both men had a good laugh. Thomas gently patted his friend on the back and said, 'Come on, my friend. Let's drink to better days'

It was on a Thursday around lunchtime on 26 February 1912 when they arrived at the Union Castle Berth in Cape Town Docks. It was a bright, sunny day with a stiff south-westerly breeze blowing across the harbour. Two Negro porters helped them load their luggage on board the *Saxon*. This ship was no stranger to them, as they had travelled on her before on past voyages to England. Once on board, the senior steward showed them to the first-class cabins. The only baggage they had with them was what was necessary for the voyage and the hotel when arriving in London. The plan was to buy themselves new clothes and any other items they would need for their coming voyage to America. Thomas would also purchase crockery, silverware, and linens for his planned hotel enterprise in Seattle. It would be shipped out with them on the *Titanic*. Once they were settled in their cabins, they decided to go up on deck for a stroll and to have their final look at Cape Town before leaving.

By around 3.30 p.m., two tugs had arrived and positioned themselves in readiness for sailing. At 4.00 exactly the ship began to move slowly away from the berth, edging her way around the rocky breakwater and finally, after releasing the tugs, heading out to the open sea. The Browns stood together on the after end of the promenade deck and for some considerable time looked back at Table Mountain. It stood out with the backdrop of a cloudless sky in all its glory in the late afternoon sunshine. It was as though they were all being given a final lasting impression of the Cape Town they have always loved as it slowly faded away in the distance. Edith asked her father if he thought they might come back one day. He said that if things went as well as planned, there was every chance they would return, if only to see old friends again.

That evening and throughout the following two days, they experienced the 'Cape Rollers,' a heavy swell and sea conditions well known by sea travellers in those regions. Many passengers were seasick, including Elizabeth. Edith and her father appeared to overcome the motion sickness and were able to go to the dining room for the evening meal. Elizabeth couldn't face food and remained in her cabin for the best part of the first two days. On the third day out, sea conditions improved, and she was soon up and about and taking food again. She began to enjoy the fine weather with the other two. Edith always remembered her mother saying that if people were going to get seasick, then they would get seasick. The only difference between first class and third class is that you pay more for the privilege!

After breakfast one morning, Thomas left his wife and daughter in deep conversation with some other ladies in one of the public rooms and made his way to the purser's office. He knew the purser from previous voyages to England; they travelled to London nearly every year to buy clothing and other items for the hotel. At that time, London was the world leader in quality goods of all descriptions and one of the best places in the world to shop. Greeting the purser like an old friend, Thomas went on to enquire as to what he might know about the new ship that would soon be arriving in Southampton called the *Titanic*. Their conversation, from what has been gathered, went something like this:

'They say she's unsinkable, according to the press,' said Thomas. 'What's you're opinion on that?'

The purser, a slightly balding man in his early fifties, looked over the top of his glasses and said, 'If you ask me, Mr Brown, I would say that the ships they are building these days are too big and one day, I shouldn't wonder, there will be a serious mishap. Apparently, the *Titanic* has been built on the same lines as her sister ship, the *Olympic*, although it's been reported that she's more luxurious. Mind you, Mr Brown, she will be a wonderful ship for passengers, but for myself, I wouldn't like to serve on her. There's talk that she will be making round trips from Southampton to New York in 16 days and with a crew of over 800. You would never get to know anyone. No, Mr Brown. She's not for the likes of me. Give me the old *Saxon* any day. It's just like one big, happy family on here, and that's a fact!'

The purser shuffled some papers on his desk and on turning, said, 'Excuse me, Mr Brown, while I just pop these bits and pieces in the safe.' With his back to Thomas, he continued the conversation. 'I hear from the chief steward, just in passing, you understand, that you and your family are hoping to sail on the *Titanic* next month if I'm not mistaken?

Thomas knew from experience that ships were always good for gossip, and the *Saxon* was no different. He didn't mind, and he felt a little proud at sailing on such a great liner as the *Titanic*. Replying to the purser, he said, 'Well, that's the plan, if the Americans don't buy all the tickets first.'

The purser said, 'That's the trouble. The Americans seem to be the only people with money these days, and they buy up everything in sight.' Just before the purser closed the safe door, Thomas caught sight of his Gladstone bag inside, which contained all of their worldly possessions. Some of those possessions included cash, jewellery, many gold sovereigns, and a few important documents. In addition, he had a money belt around his waist, and there were gold sovereigns sewn into his waistcoats and many of the women's outdoor garments. This was normal practice when wealthy people travelled in those days; it was considered the preferred and safest way to transport money. Returning to lean on his desk, the purser, now warming to the topic, went on to say how the Germans had entered the race to capture the North Atlantic trade. He thought they were building ships too quickly.

Thomas nodded slowly and said, 'Yes, yes. You may indeed be right. However, I must take my leave of you and join the ladies up on deck. It's been a pleasure talking to you. Good day.'

Before stepping out on deck, Thomas stopped by the entrance to the lobby and observed the *Saxon's* daily run chart enclosed in a glass case. He noticed that she had travelled 410 nautical miles in the past twenty-four hours, giving her a speed of 17 knots, which, Thomas thought, wasn't bad for the old girl.

As the *Saxon* continued north toward the equator, the weather improved. The swimming pool became popular among the passengers, along with a wide variety of deck games and competitions to keep them occupied. Their memories of South Africa were becoming less frequent as they continued to enjoy the balmy tropical nights. A week after crossing the equator, they were able to see the coast of West Africa and later passed the township of Dakar. Several days after that, they dropped anchor off of Las Palmas in the Canary Islands, where the ship picked up mail and provisions. From a bumboat alongside, Thomas bought some trinkets and castanets for Edith and a jewel box for Elizabeth. After just a few hours, the *Saxon* weighed anchor and proceeded on her voyage north. The weather over the next few days became colder. It was still winter in the northern hemisphere, and the Bay of Biscay made life on board uncomfortable for a couple of days until they entered the English Channel. The voyage was coming to an end. On their last night they could see St Catherine's Lighthouse and the lights of Weymouth and Bournemouth along the coastline. The *Saxon* berthed right on schedule at berth forty-six on a cold March morning.

On disembarkation, the Browns made their way to Southampton Railway Station, where they caught a train to Waterloo. On arrival in London, they caught a hackney cab. Going over Waterloo Bridge, they passed Lancaster Place, went on to The Strand, in to Aldwych, and then along Southampton Row, finally stopping in Russell Square outside of the Russell Hotel, where a porter came out to meet them.

Once settled into their hotel, Thomas spent the next few days booking their voyage on the *Titanic* and organising the shipment of hotel items to be loaded on board the ship in Southampton Docks. He managed to purchase tickets in the second class. The booking clerk told him that the second class on the *Titanic* was as good as the first class on many other transatlantic liners. After arranging all that was necessary for their voyage to America, the next plan was to get them completely fitted out in new clothes. They shopped in Knightsbridge, Mayfair, and Chelsea, Elizabeth and Edith purchasing wool serge, high-necked, and full-length fitted coats, along with double-breasted full-length coats with velvet cuffs and lapels. They bought hats to match, some with feathers, some with nets, and others with wide brims. They both had a passion for calf-length, button-up leather boots, which were very fashionable at that time. Thomas did the bulk of his shopping in Jermyn Street, St James's. He bought several custom-made tailored suits on Saville Row. With his top hat and tails and silver-topped walking cane, he looked every bit the gentleman he was.

The three of them thoroughly enjoyed themselves over these last few days, looking around the shops and setting themselves up for their new lives in America. Their stay at the Russell Hotel was a pleasant experience. Unlike other hotels of similar standing, there always appeared to be a genuine friendliness with the staff and no sign of snobbery. Thomas knew several of them from previous visits, and nothing was ever too much trouble for them. He always enjoyed chatting to some of the quick-witted Cockneys working there and would comment to Elizabeth on how there was never a dull moment with them around! Whilst staying at the hotel, Elizabeth and her daughter spent a great deal of time reading the many books in the glass cabinets scattered around in one of the lounges. The rest of the time, they were out sightseeing the places of interest around London they had yet not seen.

The weather was fine for the time of the year, inviting them out for pleasant walks along Southampton Row and Bloomsbury Park. The buds were breaking out on the plants and trees, and there was a feeling of spring in the air. Edith enjoyed the walks, as they gave her an opportunity to wear some of her new clothes and to look at other fashionable ladies walking with their gentlemen in the park. One afternoon after a visit to the British Museum, they returned to the hotel and sat in one of the lounges, reading the latest newspapers stories on the *Titanic*. There were many exaggerated stories on her interiors and spaciousness, but the general opinion was that she was an unsinkable luxury liner, and her passengers would be pampered all the way to New York.

One article stated that Bruce Ismay, the White Star Line director, would be travelling on the ship along with the ship's chief designer,

Thomas Andrews. There was also a list of the rich and famous who would be joining the ship in Southampton and Cherbourg, and it all made impressive reading. 'She's a wonderful ship, ain't she, sir?' said a waiter, noticing the full-page spread of Thomas's newspaper on the table as he set down a tray with tea and biscuits.

'She certainly is, by all accounts,' replied Thomas as he removed the newspaper from the table in order to make room for the crockery.

'Beggin' your pardon, sir, but I understand that you and your good ladies will soon be sailing on this wonder of the high seas, if I'm not mistaken?' said the waiter.

'Yes, that's correct.' Thomas was thinking how news travels, not only on ships, but in hotels as well. He had made a brief mention of their plans to the assistant manager on arrival.

Elizabeth looked at her husband, breaking out in a smile as though she'd read his thoughts. Edith, smiling to herself, continued to flick through the pages of a paper she was reading. She always remembered this conversation. Years later, retelling the story still made her laugh.

During their last few days in London, they visited the Royal Opera House, Hampton Court Palace, the Botanical Gardens at Kew, and the Tower of London. There was still much to see and time was running short, but they had managed to visit they most wanted to see. It was now 9 April, and tomorrow they would be travelling down to Southampton to join the *Titanic*. It was decided that they would spend the rest of their time enjoying the comforts the hotel had to offer and have an early night in preparation for their big day tomorrow.

Edith could never ever remember seeing her mother and father as happy as they had appeared over the past few days, chatting and laughing as they discussed their future. Edith, at 15 years of age, was taking more of an interest in things. She wanted to know what the social life would be like on board the *Titanic*. She wanted to know if there was going to be nightly entertainment. Was there an orchestra on board? If so, did they just perform for the first class? Elizabeth remarked on the coverage in the newspapers. She said there appeared to be much to do on board for everyone. Hopefully, Edith would meet several other young ladies her age. That evening, Thomas went into the bar after dinner to have his usual brandy and cigar, leaving both women chatting to other women in the lounge over coffee. They had an early morning call at six. After dressing, they went down to the dining saloon for their pre-arranged breakfast. They ate well and, after doing their final packing, went down to the lobby to arrange for their other baggage to be carried out to a waiting cab. Thomas said his farewells to some of the staff, pressing coins into their hands as they shook hands to say goodbye and wish them all bon voyage. The cab spluttered into life amid clouds of blue smoke and began its journey down Southampton Row. It was a beautiful spring morning as they motored past Bloomsbury Park on their way to Waterloo Station, chatting about how much they had enjoyed their stay at the Russell Hotel. It was a time in their lives they would never forget, but they had greater things to look forward to as they made their way to Waterloo Station. Thomas would have pulled out his gold pocket watch on its chain several times on the way, being punctual himself and checking that they were on time.

On arrival at Waterloo, a porter met them, loaded their luggage on to a cart, and then walked along the platform with them to their carriage. There were many groups of people standing along the length of the platform as the porter led them to their first-class compartments. There was the occasional whiff of coal smoke and steam from the engine, just a few carriages along, as a gentle breeze swirled about the station. The porter put their luggage into the carriage compartment; the smaller items were placed in the luggage nets above the seats. After tipping the porter for his efforts, they sorted themselves out and settled down for the journey. Soon after, there was the final slamming of carriage doors, followed by a prolonged whistle from the guard and a slight jerky movement forward. They were on their way.

As they gathered speed, they began to clear greater London, and the buildings and bridges became fewer as they headed into the countryside. Thomas would have no doubt been pondering on what might be in store for them once they arrived in Seattle. He had mentioned to Elizabeth, and to some of his business associates back in Cape Town, that the Pacific Northwest was fast becoming an important financial centre. With the Alaskan gold rush and the opening of the Panama Canal, the hotel business should do extremely well, all things being equal. With this in mind, he would have concluded that it was the right thing to do for all three of them and that they had much to look forward to.

Elizabeth, sitting alongside her husband, would have had thoughts of her own about the coming trip on the *Titanic* and the many interesting people that would be travelling with them. She wondered about the shipboard gossip that was normal on big passenger liners, and she smiled to herself. The gossip could be extremely interesting, especially from the wide range of social classes on board. Of course, it could all be taken with a large pinch of salt.

Edith sat opposite her mother and father and spent a great deal of time looking out of the window at the beautiful Berkshire and Hampshire countryside. Her thoughts were on what the future might hold for her. She would be 16 in October. Would she continue at school, or help with their new hotel enterprise? Her fate would be in the hands of her parents. She wondered if there would be any dancing on board in the evening, giving her an opportunity to wear some of the pretty dresses her parents had bought for her in London. She was also hoping there might be some other people her own age on the ship. Perhaps they could become friends. For Edith, it was going to be a completely new way of life. At times, she was finding it difficult to contain her excitement.

The train continued its journey, passing Winchester, England's ancient capital. They arrived on the outskirts of Southampton and slowed down as they entered the Northam goods yards. Southampton had a long tradition of providing the crews for the many great liners using the port, and many of the crew of the *Titanic* would have come from this district of Northam. The train slowed down as it approached Southampton's Terminus Station, passing the South Western Hotel, where many of the *Titanic's* passengers would have spent the night before boarding the ship.

The train crossed the road as it entered the Southampton Docks, winding its way through dock land and heading toward berth forty-three. Edith was full of excitement as she leaned out of the carriage window in an effort to catch sight of the huge liner everyone was talking about. She saw several ships in the docks. Finally, looking ahead, she could see the huge, black hull of the *Titanic* rising out of the water. 'There she is!' exclaimed Edith excitedly, pointing towards the Titanic as the train, now moving at walking pace, drew ever closer to the passenger sheds.

Thomas leant over his daughter to look out the window for himself before saying, 'Yes. That's her.'

Elizabeth looked out between them both and exclaimed, 'My God! She's enormous!'

They now had an excellent view of the *Titanic*. She looked serene lying alongside of the berth, her white superstructure towering over everything on the dockside and dwarfing the cranes working her cargos. Her four great, buff-coloured funnels stood proudly above everything else; smoke curling lazily from their black shiny tops. It was indeed a breathtaking sight for those on the train, peering out of the windows and seeing this mighty liner for the very first time.

Once inside the great cargo and passenger shed, the train came to a halt, puffing, wheezing, and blowing steam and smoke everywhere around the front end of the engine. Inside, the terminal was a hive of activity with passengers and dockworkers milling about. Carts and baggage moved to and fro around the great shed and to the ships' gangways. A porter helped them get their luggage to the second-class gangway as Thomas pulled out his pocket watch to note that the time was 10.20 a.m. They had made good time from London. As the ship wasn't due to sail until noon, he thought they would have plenty of time to settle into their cabins and then look around the ship. At the foot of the gangway before boarding, Thomas produced his tickets and some documents regarding the hotel items sent earlier. He enquired if those items had been loaded yet. He was assured that everything was in order, and Elizabeth led the way up the gangway with Edith following and Thomas behind them both.

Looking up at the white superstructure high above them, they could see rows of portholes with the morning sunshine glinting on their brass rims. Higher up, they could see passengers leaning on the ship's rail, shouting down now and then to friends and loved ones on the dockside. As they continued up the slight slope of the gangway to the open shell doors at the top, Thomas became faint and his legs began to buckle. Clutching on to the handrail, he tried to remain on his feet.

Elizabeth, turning around realising something was wrong, pushed past Edith and grabbed hold of his arm. 'What on earth is the matter, Tom?' she said nervously. 'You're shaking!' she said, more in alarm than anything else. 'What's come over you?'

Thomas, wiping his brow and regaining his feet, said shakily, 'I don't know, my dear.' Regaining his composure, he said, 'I think I'm over it now. Let's get on board.'

Both women turned around and started up again, finally entering the plush foyer on board the ship at the top of the gangway.

Once on board, they immediately took in the plush carpeting and beautiful wood panelling around the entrance lobby. Crossing over to the purser's office, Thomas, now feeling somewhat recovered, deposited his Gladstone bag with its gold sovereigns, bank notes, and jewellery. They were promptly assigned to a steward, who politely asked then to follow as he led them to their cabins on E Deck. They fell in behind him as they went along the passageway with its varnished handrails and oak panelling on either side. The smell of newness was everywhere. They went down two flights of stairs to arrive outside of the ladies' cabin after a short walk. After opening the door for them, the steward led Thomas a bit further along the passageway to the two-berth cabin he would be sharing with another gentleman.

Both women were well pleased with their accommodation. The bunks, one above the other, were made up with big white pillows, crisp white sheets, and decorative counterpanes with the White Star logo in the centre. The floor of the cabin was beautifully carpeted, and there were two comfortable chairs, a washstand and mirror, fluffy white towels, and water jugs and glasses. The bunks had curtains that could be drawn right across, and there were neat little curtains at the porthole. Thomas returned from his cabin, which was identical to theirs, to see how the ladies were getting on and to help with some of the luggage. Elizabeth asked her husband if he was feeling any better after his near-collapse on the gangway.

He said he couldn't understand what had come over him. Stopping what he was doing for a moment, he said thoughtfully, 'I felt like that in Cape Town, if I remember rightly, when booking the passage on the *Saxon*. I just don't understand it. However, I feel fine now, so let's sort this out later and go up on deck.'

Making their way up to the open decks, they passed many passengers in the passageways sorting out their baggage and being directed to their cabins by fussing stewards. After going along the passageways and up several flights of stairs, they arrived on the second-class promenade deck and strolled along with other groups of people. They went to the ship's rail and looked down on the dockside far below them, where throngs of people milled about as cranes swung their cargos into the ship's holds.

They continued their walk around the decks. Whilst up on the boat deck, they noticed much more smoke coming out of the funnels than what they had first seen when arriving on the train. There was also much more steam coming out of the waste pipes at the top of the funnels. The *Titanic* was preparing for sea.

CHAPTER THREE

TITANIC DAY ONE

Captain Smith would have arrived on board the *Titanic* around 7.30 a.m. on sailing day after travelling from his home in Winn Road, Southampton. The crew was to be mustered at 8.00, and he would have a busy morning right up until sailing at noon. There would have been many visitors to his cabin, including the chief engineer, port officials, senior officers, and the Board of Trade. After crew muster that morning, there was a boat drill, and two boats were lowered into the water. Around nine men manned these boats, rowing around the immediate dock area and testing some of the gear. Coaling of the ship had been completed, with coal having been taken from the White Star ships *Oceanic* and *Majestic*.

Both ships had been laid up due to a national coal strike, which had ended just a few days ago. Down in the boiler rooms, firemen had been kept busy by a fire that had developed in no.10 bunker. They were hosing down the coal and shovelling hot cinders away from the seat of the fire. Fires were not uncommon in coal-burning ships during bunkering, which were sometimes caused by friction and atomised coal dust. These bunkers were in restricted areas, and keeping the fires contained would have been difficult to say the least. A close eye was kept on the situation, with extra men being deployed to that section to keep things under control.

Able Seaman Fred Fleet was a lookout man. He had served in that capacity when the ship came down from the builder's yard in Belfast. He had binoculars then, but after arrival in Southampton they had gone missing from the crow's-nest. They would have been used for the ship's trials in the crow's-nest over the measured mile, to study the ship's manoeuvrability, and to keep an eye out for other shipping around whilst this was going on. It's doubtful that binoculars would have been issued to lookouts once the ship commenced its service runs to the US.

The Board of Trade would have issued certificates as regards to the ship's seaworthiness and that the sixteen lifeboats would accommodate 910 persons, along with the two accident boats accommodating a further 80 persons. The four collapsible boats were capable of holding 188 persons, giving a total life-saving capacity of 1,178 people for all lifeboats. This meant that there was only enough life-saving equipment for just over half the total of 2,200 passengers and crew. With this discrepancy in life-saving equipment, the *Titanic* was to sail across the Atlantic after calling in at Cherbourg in France and Queenstown in Ireland.

Throughout the morning on sailing day, the dockside was a hive of activity, with many more dockworkers, passengers, and well-wishers arriving and much jostling around the foot of the gangways.

When huge liners prepared for sailing, there was usually a carnival atmosphere in the port, and Edith described the scene many times when talking about leaving Southampton that day on the *Titanic*. Shore personnel seemed to be forever going up and down the three gangways, carrying boxes, packages, and flowers. Members of the crew would have been going up the forward crew gangway with their kit, and there would also have been those who had been to The Grapes pub for their last drink ashore before sailing.

This was traditional for all seamen before sailing, and it's understood that, upon returning to the ship, some were turned away for being too late to go on watch. Others, waiting around for such an opportunity, would have taken their places. Such were those times of high unemployment. Those who had lost their jobs on the dockside were not to know at the time that their last drinks ashore and the loss of their jobs had possibly saved their lives.

It was at the forward gangway that many of the single male passengers would have their accommodation. They, too, would be boarding the ship with whatever belongings they had at the time. Finally, a crane swung its jib around and a sling was attached to the gangways in readiness to lift them away as sailing time approached.

Thomas, Elizabeth, and Edith were watching all of this activity from one of the upper decks and were fascinated at everything that was going on below them. They had been allowed to explore some of the first-class decks before sailing, and were most impressed by what they had seen. They later ventured on to the boat deck. It was here that many were caught by surprise by an ear-shattering blast from one of the ship's funnels. They all ducked at first, but on rising, they laughed, realising that the *Titanic* was preparing for sea.

Up on the bridge, Captain Smith would have ordered the chief officer to have the forward gangway removed and the boatswain to call the men to stations. Within ten minutes of the ship's whistle echoing around the port of Southampton, three tugs, the *Hector, Neptune*, and *Vulcan*, arrived off of berth forty-three in readiness to take up their towing positions.

White Star Line's choice pilot, Captain Bowyer, was one of a long line of Bowyers who still pilot ships out of Southampton today. He had arrived on the bridge with a junior officer and immediately shook hands with Captain Smith, saying, 'Good morning, Captain. How was your run down from Belfast?'

'Fine,' replied the captain. 'She did all that was asked of her and briefly touched 24 knots on the measured mile.' Then he added, 'We don't intend to push her on this voyage, but if the weather is on our side, she could do well with her cruising speed.'

The pilot, nodding his head in an understanding way, walked over to the binnacle and checked the reading on the compass to a fixed marker ashore.

The *Titanic* sailed some twenty minutes late due to the late arrival of the last boat train. As the ship's moorings were being let go, the tugs assisting began to pull her off of the dockside, the gap slowly widening between ship and shore. Streamers were being stretched to their limits as passengers threw flowers to those on the quayside amid shouts and waving. The ship's orchestra continued to play lively music.

Thomas, Elizabeth, and Edith said little, but they waved along with everyone else, just enjoying the wonderful atmosphere as the ship slowly moved away from berth forty-three. Once the ship was clear of the berth, people ashore could be seen walking along the dockside to keep pace with her as the tugs finally helped her around in the swinging ground to face seaward.

From the wing of *Titanic's* bridge, the pilot indicated further towing positions to the tugs by way of a mouth whistle, finally releasing them from their towing tasks with a series of whistles and sometimes a wave. The only tug now assisting *Titanic* was the lead tug, just keeping the towing wire taut to *Titanic's* bow as it led the great ship out of the port. Captain Smith would have given the engine room the order to proceed at slow ahead until clearing the dock area. There would be considerable turbulence under her counter stern as her three mighty bronze propellers churned up the water as she headed downstream. Caution with speed would be exercised until the vessel was clear of the docks, as there is usually a speed limit within all dock areas.

As the *Titanic* gathered way, just ahead of her, at Dock Head, two ships were moored together side by side. This was sometimes known as being double-banked. The two ships were the *New York* and the *Oceanic*, and as the *Titanic* came almost abeam of them, the outboard vessel, the *New York,* parted some moorings and drifted toward the *Titanic* due to a displacement surge from the larger vessel under way. The deep-water channel from the buoy 'Gymp Elbow' off of berth forty-three to Dock Head would have been restricted in 1912. A huge liner would have caused the canal effect, as it's known, if a ship's speed had not been kept down until clearing the docks. For the *Titanic* to have picked up enough speed in such a short distance to cause such a displacement surge from the swinging ground is difficult to understand.

All ships leaving the Western Docks make a course alteration off of berth thirty-eight to steer for a course to the Hook buoy off of Fawley. Although the course alteration is not great, it will increase a displacement problem if the rate of knots is not kept down. At this point, 'slow with caution' should have been observed until clear of Dock Head. The more likely reason for the outboard ship to break away when the *Titanic* approached was that she wasn't moored up properly for double banking. She should have remained alongside as the larger vessel passed. The tug *Vulcan*, being in attendance to the *Titanic*, managed to avert a serious incident by towing the *New York* out of harm's way and back alongside the berth.

At this stage, Captain Smith had ordered a full astern command to the engine room, which responded immediately, as they were still on standby mode from sailing. The engine rooms on ships should always be on standby until the pilot leaves.

The Browns had witnessed the incident, and Thomas once again became pale. He told Edith that it was a bad omen for a ship to sail late and then almost collide before leaving the docks. Thomas, still appearing a bit shaken, continued to stare at the *New York* as she was towed out of danger by the tug *Vulcan*.

Once the *New York* was well clear, Captain Smith gave the order of half ahead on all engines as the *Titanic* started to move forward again, down Southampton Water toward the Solent. It's true to say that superstitions related to the sea ran deep in those days, and many of the crew had also mentioned the bad luck of sailing late on a maiden voyage.

Once out of Southampton Water and going around Calshot Spit, the *Titanic* entered the Thorn Channel, rounded the West Brambles buoy, and headed for Mother Bank and the Nab Tower, where the pilot would disembark. On occasions when the sea was rough, pilots would remain on board and leave the ship at Cherbourg, but on this day, 10 April 1912, the weather was fine. At 2 p.m., the pilot cutter drew alongside to let the pilot off. Once clear, Captain Smith ordered all engines full ahead, and the *Titanic* steamed across the English Channel and headed for Cherbourg.

Many of the passengers who had been on deck when the ship left Southampton were now seated in their respective dining saloons, enjoying lunch, their first meal of the voyage.

In the second-class dining saloon, the Browns had Rev. Earnest Carter and his wife, Lillian, as dining companions, and they soon learned from each other their business for being on the voyage. The Carters were from a small parish just outside of London. They had planned this trip for years, as they had never been out of England before. Thomas mentioned his business interests in South Africa and the forthcoming hotel enterprise he was hoping to start in Seattle. Both men got on extremely well, as did the ladies, and they remained good friends throughout the voyage.

After their wonderful lunch in the dining saloon, which gave them a foretaste of the superb cuisine yet to come, the Browns set off for further walks around the ship. They visited the library, with its beautiful wood panelling, well-stocked shelves of books, and comfortable armchairs. Attractive standard lamps were placed around the room. Elizabeth and Edith, avid readers, were delighted with the wide range of books, knowing they would be spending many pleasant hours here during their voyage.

Thomas was well pleased with the smoking room. It had comfortable seating, card tables, and a bar at one end, all of which, he thought, had the atmosphere typical of a gentleman's club in London. Back out on deck, the three of them found it too chilly and breezy to stay for long.

The ship was now making her own wind as she ploughed across the English Channel at 20 knots. During the short voyage across to Cherbourg, afternoon tea was served in one of the second-class public rooms. On a grander scale, high tea was being served in the first-class lounge, with a classical selection being played by a string quartet from the ship's orchestra.

The *Titanic* arrived outside of Cherbourg at 6.30 p.m. and dropped anchor in the harbour. Passengers were to be brought out to the ship by two tenders. Those two ferries, named *Traffic* and *Nomadic*, were built by Harland and Wolff for White Star Line specifically for this type of work. Many passengers began to gather on deck to watch the arrival of the two tenders, the first one alongside bringing the first-class passengers; the other tender with second- and third-class passengers on board. Among the 142 first-class passengers boarding from the first tender were some well-known and wealthy people of the time. More passengers, thirty for second class and around a hundred for third class, boarded from the second tender. In addition to their baggage, there was also a great quantity of mail to be loaded. Once on board, it was taken straight to the mailroom for sorting.

At 8 p.m., Captain Smith gave the orders to weigh anchor as the tenders pulled away from the ship. Once clear, they gave the *Titanic* three toots on their whistles to wish the vessel 'Bon voyage.' The liner responded with three thunderous blasts from her own whistles, which must have been heard all over Cherbourg. Once the anchor was weighed, the *Titanic*, with deck lights and pinhole lights showing from her portholes, slowly turned away from the lights of Cherbourg and headed into the darkness of the English Channel. With her four massive funnels floodlit, she would have made a spectacular sight to onlookers ashore.

Of the rich and famous on board, there was Isodor Strauss and his wife, Ida, owners of the well-known Macy's department stores in America. They always travelled abroad with her maid and his valet. There was also John Jacob Astor with his young wife, Madeleine, just half his age, and Bruce Ismay, the White Star Line's managing director, who was occupying one of the staterooms and travelling with his valet and secretary. Thomas Andrews, the ship's designer, was in a first-class cabin, although this would be a working voyage for him.

There were also several shipyard technicians, brought along on the maiden voyage to iron out any problems that might arise on this first trip across the Atlantic. This was normal procedure for a ship of this size, and the 'guarantee group,' as they were sometimes known, were usually well employed on these 'shakedown' voyages. This group of men would have been there when her keel was laid, and they knew practically every rivet that had gone into her construction. They had been there at the start and had helped to build her. They knew her as a 'good job' and were proud to be sailing with her on her maiden voyage.

In the third class, many of the emigrants who had boarded at Cherbourg had travelled long distances through France and Eastern Europe. They were glad of a good meal and some well earned sleep.

In the second-class library, Edith and her mother were feeling the effects of a very long day and had decided to turn in for the night. They were escorted to their cabin by Thomas, who kissed both of them and wished them a good night's sleep before returning to the smoking room for a nightcap.

The *Titanic* steamed westward throughout the night, heading for Queenstown in Southern Ireland. The fire in no. ten bunker was still burning. Despite their efforts, the stokers had not been able to put it out.

LUNCH MENU

R.M.S. " TITANIC "
April 14, 1912

LUNCHEON

Consomme` Fermier　　　　　Cockie Leekie

Fillets of Brill

Egg A L' Argenteuil

Chicken A La Maryland

Corned Beef, Vegetables, Dumplings

FROM THE GRILL

Grilled Mutton Chops

Mashed, Fried, & Baked Jacket Potatoes

Custard Pudding

Apple Meringue　　　　　　Pastry

BUFFET

Salmon Mayonaise　　　　Potted Shrimps

Norwegian Anchovies　　　Soused Herrings

Plain and Smoked Sardines

Roast Beef

Round of Spiced Beef

Veal & Ham Pie

Virginian & Cumberland Ham

Bologna Sausage　　　　　　Brawn

Galantine of Chicken

Corned Ox Tongue

Lettuce　　　　Beetroot　　　　Tomatoes

CHEESE

Cheshire, Stilton, Gorgonzola, Edam,

Camembert, Roqufort, St. Ivel,

Cheddar.

Iced Draught Munich Lager Beer, 3p & 6p a Tankard

CHAPTER FOUR

TITANIC DAY TWO

At daybreak on 11 April, the sea was calm with an overcast sky, but the weather was generally still mild for the time of the year off of the English coast. During the night, the *Titanic* had steamed some 240 nautical miles, had rounded Lands End on the south-western most point of the British Isles, and had entered St George's Channel later that morning. At 11.30 a.m., she had arrived just outside of Queenstown and dropped anchor off of Roches Point. For passengers with their cabins right forward in the third class, the dropping of the anchor would have been an experience few would be likely to forget. There would have been a thunderous roar as the huge links of the anchor cable (chain) scraped and banged up the spurling pipe from the anchor cable locker below. There would have been great rattling noises as the chain raced around the capstan up on deck and then crashed down the hawse pipe, following the huge anchor into the sea. It would have left them in little doubt as to why the fares for travelling in this part of the ship were the cheapest on board.

Soon after dropping anchor, two tenders could be seen coming out of the harbour and heading toward the *Titanic*. As they drew closer, it could be seen that they were paddle steamers, and once they were almost alongside, their names could be made out quite clearly. They were appropriately called the *Ireland* and the *America*, and their presence alongside saw many emigrants standing on their decks waiting to board the *Titanic*. Once moored alongside, a somewhat rickety gangway was hoisted up to the *Titanic's* shell doors, which were situated about twelve feet above the top deck of the tenders. Once secured, several port officials boarded, followed soon by the first of the passengers and their baggage. Several traders had come out with the tenders and were now on the second-class promenade deck, displaying their wares along with beautiful Irish linens. There was a young fiddler playing Irish jigs with his upturned cap on the deck by his feet. He was appreciated by many, if the coins in his cap were anything to go by.

During the *Titanic's* brief stay at Queenstown, she had taken on board a further 110 third-class passengers, six second-class passengers, and 1,400 sacks of mail. One of the seven passengers disembarking at Queenstown took a photo of Captain Smith looking down from the cab on the wing of the bridge. This was probably the last picture ever taken of him. Today, that photo would no doubt be worth a considerable amount of money to collectors of such things. The sacks of mail were taken to the mailrooms for sorting by post office employees (not White Star personnel). The sorting of mail on transatlantic liners before arrival at the port of destination was never an option, but the mail contract was much sought-after by other operators, and White Star Line had the edge on this lucrative business. With the post office workers sorting mail around the clock during the voyage, mail would be bagged up and ready for delivery on arrival to the many states in America. This would shorten delivery times throughout the United States by many days, something other competitors just couldn't match at that time.

On sailing from Queenstown, nearly all of the passengers were in their dining saloons being served lunch. A few were on deck watching the tenders leave, also giving three toots on their whistles as a bon-voyage gesture to the great liner. In acknowledgement, the *Titanic* again let forth three thunderous blasts from one of her funnels as winch gear on the forecastle castle head could be heard weighing anchor. The ship's bow swung westward and headed for the North Atlantic, slowly gathering speed on a calm grey sea. Shafts of bright sunlight broke through an overcast sky, creating silver like patches on the sea ahead as the pride of the White Star Line continued on her maiden voyage.

Edith and her father decided to go up on deck after lunch, while Elizabeth preferred to go below for a nap in her cabin. Edith, holding on to her father's arm as they strolled around the deck, asked him if he had ever met Aunt Josephine in Seattle.

'No, I haven't, as a matter of fact, my dear. But I'm really looking forward to meeting up with her and her husband and meeting new friends,' Turning to look at his daughter as they continued their walk, he asked if she was looking forward to her new life in Seattle.

'I am,' replied Edith. 'I don't know what to really expect, other than what you and mother have told me.'

They went over to the ship's rail to take in the beautiful green hills along the Irish coastline. At the stern of the ship, several passengers were looking back at the slowly fading coast of Southern Ireland, a coast that many of them would never see again.

As darkness fell, the rich and famous in the first class were preparing for cocktails, and then it was on to the dining saloon for dinner. On this first day out, Bruce Ismay would have spent some time with Thomas Andrews, discussing the ship's performance since leaving Southampton. At this point in the voyage, the great reciprocating engines would not have had ample time to settle down, and the speed of the ship on the first day's run would have been well below what could be expected over the next few days.

Thomas Brown was in the smoking room, accompanied by Rev. Carter, enjoying a drink or two before going down to escort the ladies to the second-class dining saloon.

In the third class, meals would have been served earlier than in the other classes. Afterwards, the passengers would sit in their general room or smoking room and chat about what might be in store for them on arrival in New York. Down in the engine room, engineers would no doubt be sipping tea from mugs, walking around the machinery and checking temperatures, pressure gauges, and moving parts. In the boiler rooms, it was sweat and toil all the way, with firemen stripped to the waist, shovelling never-ending quantities of coal into the roaring fires. By the time the *Titanic* would have reached New York, these men would have shovelled some 3,000 tons of coal into her hungry furnaces.

After dinner that evening, many passengers retired to the lounges to relax after being pampered for over two hours in the dining saloons.

It was here that shipboard gossip was passed around, and one would quickly find out who was who on board the ship. There would be many exaggerated tales about the wonderful ship on which they were travelling, the items that were available on board, the exquisite catering in the first-class dining saloon, and the Gattis restaurant experience.

They would talk about the Countess of Rothes, the Astors, and the Strauss family, rich American women with their funny little dogs. Everyone that was anyone would come under the microscope on this great floating city and, of course, it was a great way to pass the time in between drinks and card schools. There were many business people on board, and no doubt one or two deals could be struck before arrival in New York. Others who frequently travelled on the great transatlantic liners would be professional gamblers, although the White Star Line was not the only carrier that had that problem.

At the end of the second day at sea, the *Titanic* continued to plough through the water. White foam, lit up by the ship's lights, was forced away from the ship's side as she headed into the night. In the almost total blackness ahead, America was still a long way off. Astern of her, one or two solitary lights were still visible on the horizon.

For those on board, a very uncertain future. For most, no future at all.

CHAPTER FIVE

TITANIC DAY THREE

It was the morning of Friday, 12 April. Edith had been awake for some time, thinking about what her new life would be like in Seattle and wondering what it would be like not knowing anyone. Lying there quietly, she could hear the distant, regular throb of the engines from deep down in the ship. In the passageway outside of their cabin, there was a clink now and then of crockery from the morning tea being served. She finally sat up, pulled her blankets to one side and, turning, climbed down the little bunk ladder to the cabin floor. At the same time her mother, in the lower berth, pulled her curtains open and greeted her daughter, who was now crossing the cabin floor to look out of the porthole. Both women had slept well; they decided it was the sea air that had allowed them to 'sleep like a log,' as Elizabeth put it. Looking out of the porthole, Edith could see that it was the start of another nice day, with a calm sea and the sun trying to break through the grey early morning cloud. Both women decided to dress before Thomas arrived to take them up on deck for a morning stroll before breakfast.

After a short, brisk walk around the promenade deck, they went down below for breakfast. On entering the dining saloon they met the Carters, who had arrived at the same time. After the usual pleasantries, they all took their seats and examined the breakfast menu. Some of the choices on offer, apart from a wide range of cereals and fruit juices, were sautéed kidneys, eggs, bacon, sausages, grilled tomatoes, and fried bread. There were also American pancakes with either maple syrup or honey.

During the breakfast conversation between the two men, Rev. Carter politely asked Thomas which denomination he belonged to. The Church of England, Thomas said. He went on to say that his family had their own pew in Cape Town Cathedral and seldom missed a service. Rev. Carter said he would be offering his services to the purser for the coming Sunday evening service in the ship's library.

After breakfast, Edith and her mother decided to go to the library to take advantage of some of its interesting books and to read the newspapers that had been brought on board at Queenstown. Thomas, on the other hand, decided to take a good long walk around the boat deck to work off the big breakfast he had just eaten and to get some sea air into his lungs. Once on the upper decks, he noticed that it was colder than the day before, but he considered that to be normal now that they were further out to sea and well away from the land. On his walk, he noticed a ship's officer climbing down from the ship's master compass platform, which was situated between the second and third funnels. Thomas decided this was an opportune moment to enquire about the ship's arrival in New York. He asked whether the ship would be trying to beat her sister ship, the *Olympic*, on her run across the Atlantic. Would the ship arrive any earlier than advertised? The officer, replying carefully, said that the ship was not out to break any records. It would be up to the captain and chief engineer if they saw fit. Besides, it was not company policy to drive their ships too hard on maiden voyages. The officer finally quipped, 'Better to play safe and arrive on time than not to arrive at all!'

Thomas, with one of his well-known little chuckles, replied, 'One couldn't ask for more.' He wished the officer a pleasant day as he continued his walk around the boat deck.

In the ship's library, Edith and her mother were engrossed in their reading when another woman came over to them and started up a conversation with Elizabeth. Edith overheard the woman saying, 'Do you know, there's something about this ship that I find very unsettling.'

Elizabeth, quite a nervous person at the best of times, looked at her anxiously and asked, 'In what way?'

The woman replied, 'Quite frankly, I can't put my finger on it. But when we were in Queenstown, I felt a kind of panic. I wanted my husband to cancel the remainder of the voyage and get me off.'

Edith remembered this conversation throughout her life. She always maintained that the woman in question did look a bundle of nerves. The woman went on to say that she and her husband had travelled the Atlantic before, and she had usually been able to settle down after a day or two, but not on the *Titanic*.

Elizabeth continued to listen intently as the woman went on. 'Since I've been on this ship, I haven't slept a wink, and I just feel uneasy the whole time. Although, one must admit, she's a beautiful ship for all of that.'

Elizabeth, appearing a little troubled herself, finally added, 'I do hope you get a good night's sleep and settle down a bit better as the trip goes on.'

Edith and her mother never saw the woman again throughout the remainder of the voyage and never knew what became of her.

The purser's office is the one place on a passenger ship that everyone visits at one time or another during the voyage, as all passengers' requirements are controlled from there. Apart from offering a banking service on board, it is also the information centre for the entire vessel. It was here that Thomas would visit around midday to study the ship's run details and to take part in the daily sweepstake on predicting the daily mileage. Since leaving Queenstown, the *Titanic* had logged 385 nautical miles. This was well short of the predicted day's run, but it was to be expected this early in the voyage, after only steaming for twenty-two hours. This meant that her average speed had only been 17 knots, and everyone knew she would be doing better than that in the days to come.

In the lounges, there was talk that the ship might reach New York on the evening of Tuesday, 16 April, instead of the next day, as scheduled, although passengers would have to remain on board until the morning. This would mean that her estimated time of arrival would be some twelve hours sooner than advertised, giving the White Star Line the edge on all other carriers. This would do wonders for the mail contract and the company's prestige internationally. All of this being achieved on a brand-new liner on her maiden voyage was a real possibility, and with the unseasonably good weather to help her along, it would have been tempting for the captain and crew to go for it.

There was also talk on the ship about a vibration which was beginning to be felt in some of the lower deck cabins aft. Marine engineers have always known that huge liners needed a day or two to settle down to reach their cruising speeds. Weather permitting, and without adding extra coal to the furnaces, these ships would improve on their speed each day.

Whilst in the library, Edith and Elizabeth took up a conversation with a middle-aged couple. The topic under discussion was how young some of the bellboys looked. The middle-aged man appeared to know that they were employed at the age of fourteen, much the same as the hotel industry ashore. He went on to say that it was perhaps the only opportunity they would ever have to see the world.

On entering the library a little later, Thomas joined the group. After a further period of small talk, he heard the man mention a fire down in the ship's bunkers. The man said, 'Did you know that since leaving Southampton, there's been a fire raging down in the stoke hole and, up to this moment in time, they are still unable to put it out?'

This was the last thing Thomas wanted to hear with Elizabeth standing beside him. This revelation wasn't going to do her nerves any good at all.

The man went on. 'Our saloon steward has a friend who is a stoker on board, and he told him they are still deploying extra men down there to try and keep it under control.'

Thomas tried to play it down a bit by saying, 'I'm sure it's under control. Besides, ships being what they are for gossip, it's fairly certain that more people would have heard about it by now.'

The overweight, middle-aged man was not to be deterred. 'That may be so, but it doesn't fill one with much confidence in the White Star Line, does it?' His wife, a huge woman, nodded at every word her husband was saying, looking first at Elizabeth, then to Thomas, and then back to her husband. Thomas, realising a rapid escape was necessary, quickly told them that they must take their leave, as they were about to meet others for tea in one of the lounges.

That evening after retiring to their cabin, Elizabeth and Edith noticed, for the first time, vibration around their cabin. This was evident by a slight rattle from the door handle now and then, the clink of glasses on the washstand, and the occasional creak from the wood panelling. These were sounds they had not noticed before. Edith quickly turned in for the night, although she was aware of her mother sitting below her on the edge of her bunk for some time before turning in herself. Knowing her mother to be quite nervous, Edith wondered if she was still worried about the earlier conversation about the fire in the ship's bunkers. Drawing her curtains across her upper berth, Edith turned out her bunk light and lay quietly, listening to the throb of the ship's engines deep within the vessel as she fell asleep.

CHAPTER SIX

TITANIC DAY FOUR

It was Saturday, 13 April. The weather continued to be unusually fine for that time of the year in the North Atlantic. Before breakfast and before the change of the watch, Captain Smith would have arrived in the wheelhouse to go over the charts with the chief officer. There would have been the usual talk about weather conditions, wet and dry temperatures, ship revolutions, the latest fix, and the speed estimate. All radio reports and the general running of the vessel during the night would have been discussed, and, of course, the progress down below with the bunker fire. It was reported that the fire was out, although the situation would continue to be monitored. Captain Smith would have left the chartroom, asking to be informed if anything untoward cropped up, and he would have made his way down to breakfast.

The ship's post office and mailrooms were situated well down at waterline level on G Deck. The postal workers down there had a mammoth task ahead of them, sorting out mail from hundreds of huge sacks before arrival in New York. The General Post Office in the UK employed the mail sorters. It was considered to be a job with a difference. It was much sought-after by postal workers who wanted to be able to visit America whilst doing their mundane jobs as sorters.

Captain Smith visited the second-class deck at around ten that morning on one of his public relations exercises for the White Star Line. Many big passenger-shipping companies had a policy that the ship's master would visit all classes during the voyage and to talk to passengers. As he stopped to chat now and then with some passengers, he looked to be in a jovial mood. Smartly dressed in his full drape, navy blue jacket with four gold rings around each cuff, he looked a fine figure of a man. Under his cap, with gold braid around its peak, was a kindly, round face. His clipped white beard gave the impression of everyone's favourite grandfather. With his sharply creased, navy blue trousers and shiny black shoes, he looked every bit the captain of the world's most famous liner.

During this walk around the boat deck, Captain Smith stopped at the Browns, who were sitting in deck chairs. Edith never forgot the conversation that followed. The captain asked them all if they were enjoying the voyage. Thomas answered for them, saying that sailing on the *Titanic* had been a most enjoyable experience, especially on her maiden voyage.

Captain Smith then turned his attention to Edith. Smiling, he asked, 'And how about you, young lady?'

Edith, first looking at her mother and then back to the captain, said, 'It's the best ship we've ever been on.'

Captain Smith, laughing at that, said he was glad to hear it. Edith then asked if there were dogs on board the ship. The captain said the ship did have dogs on board, and that the chief butcher usually looked after them. They can be exercised on one of the upper decks (known by the crew as the 'dog deck,' and it was situated up by one of the funnels).

Edith asked the captain if he had a dog. He said he did. 'But not on board ship, I hasten to add. He's back home in Southampton, where he should be. When I get back to Southampton after this voyage, I shall have more time to spend with him.'

Thomas changed the subject, asking Captain Smith if the ship was running to schedule. The captain replied that the ship was making good time with the excellent weather so far, and they should reach New York at the time advertised. He said it would get colder over the next couple of days, but that was to be expected in those waters at that time of the year. With that, he gave them all a half salute and wished them a pleasant day.

At noon, the ship's position was fixed. It was shown that she had travelled some 518 nautical miles since noon the previous day, giving her an average speed of 21 knots. This was well within the expectations of her service speed, which had been estimated by her designers to be 24 knots, after a shakedown period. By late afternoon on this day, the *Titanic* had reached the halfway point in crossing the Atlantic and was well on time for arrival in New York.

One of Thomas's favourite places to visit on board was the smoking room, where many of the gentlemen liked to have a chat and puff away on their pipes or cigars. Women never ventured there. There was nothing to say they shouldn't, but it was considered 'not the done thing.' They preferred, instead, to gather in the reading or writing rooms and talk about the things that women liked to talk about. It was during that Saturday afternoon that one of the gentlemen talking to Thomas and Rev. Carter mentioned that ice was of concern to some of the ship's navigating officers.

This information apparently came to this particular gentleman when the question of icebergs came up during a brief conversation the previous day. The officer had told him in a casual way that officers who had travelled the North Atlantic on previous crossings were a bit concerned about the mild winter in the north. Mild winters are rare events, but when they occur, more ice breaks away in the spring and drifts south with the currents. This had been discussed several times in the officer's wardroom during the voyage, and they were fully aware of this phenomenon. At the end of their conversation, the officer assured the gentleman that there would be no danger to a ship like the *Titanic*, with her watertight compartments and sophisticated radio equipment.

That evening after dinner, Thomas went to the smoking room to meet up with the other gentlemen there, playing cards and drinking a brandy or two after the meal. The conversation would have been the usual business talk, with world affairs in general under discussion.

The ladies retired to the lounge. There would have been some dancing, probably in the first class, although Edith did remember one or two nights when part of the orchestra performed in the second class as well. The third class would have entertained themselves, much as they had always done. At this stage of the voyage, they would have been full of anticipation of their future prospects and thoughts of home.

TRIPLE SCREW STEAMER "TITANIC."

2ND CLASS

APRIL 14, 1912.

DINNER.

CONSOMMÉ TAPIOCA

BAKED HADDOCK, SHARP SAUCE

CURRIED CHICKEN & RICE

SPRING LAMB, MINT SAUCE

ROAST TURKEY, CRANBERRY SAUCE

GREEN PEAS   PUREE TURNIPS

BOILED RICE

BOILED & ROAST POTATOES

PLUM PUDDING

WINE JELLY   COCOANUT SANDWICH

AMERICAN ICE CREAM

NUTS ASSORTED

FRESH FRUIT

CHEESE   BISCUITS

COFFEE

CHAPTER SEVEN

TITANIC DAY FIVE

Sunday, 14 April, started much the same as the previous few days for Elizabeth and her daughter, with Elizabeth on that occasion being first out of bed and peering out of the porthole. On returning to her bunk, she noticed Edith stirring and apologised if she had woken her. She went on to mention that the sea remained calm and the weather fine. A short time later, Thomas tapped on their door as usual, to let them know that he was up and about and would be waiting for them to join him up on deck for their early morning walk. They enjoyed their regular walks about the decks before breakfast in order to get some sea air and an appetite before going down to the dining saloon. Once up on deck, they soon realised that, despite the calm weather, it was much colder outside; certainly the coldest day of the voyage so far. After a brisk walk around the boat deck, they decided they should go below before they got any colder.

In the dining saloon, several other passengers commented on the drop in temperature. Others spoke again about the vibration being felt in some cabins during the night. Rev. Carter was under the impression that the ship gathered speed at night, when everyone was asleep, and returned to the normal cruising speed at daybreak.

On the bridge at nine o'clock, an ice report was received from the Cunard Line vessel *Caronia*, reporting an ice field 42 degrees north to longitude, 50 degrees west. This gave a position ahead of the *Titanic*, but to starboard, and not on her track. At noon, the ship's position was worked out and the distance logged since noon the previous day (ships' days start and end at noon each day). The distance steamed was 545 nautical miles, giving her a speed of almost 23 knots, a speed expected at this stage in the voyage. The air temperature at that time was 48 degrees and steady.

At eleven o'clock, a Church of England service was held in the second-class dining saloon, conducted by the assistant purser. The third class was also invited to attend if they wished. A service was also held at this time in one of the first-class public rooms, conducted by Captain Smith. After the Sunday services, many passengers chose to stay below decks to keep out of the cold, the ship's rate of knots creating a considerable wind chill up on the open decks. At 1.40 p.m., White Star Line's east bound liner, the *Baltic*, reported ice in a similar position to that reported earlier by the *Caronia*. Five minutes later, the ship *Amerika* reported ice, again in the same position as the earlier reports. These ice reports suggested quite clearly that a huge ice field was drifting south with the current. This was not unusual in those areas, but it was something to watch out for as the ship continued on her course.

At 5.45 p.m., Captain Smith was on the bridge for the expected course alteration that would take them some sixteen nautical miles further south than their intended course. Studying the charts and the ice reports that had reached the bridge, he reckoned that their course alteration should steer them well clear of the reported ice field. At that time, the air temperature had dropped 3 degrees, and the sea temperature was down to 33 degrees.

Before dinner that evening, the Browns decided to brave the cold and went up on deck to witness a calm, almost glass-like sea and a beautiful sunset. Once again it was too cold to remain up there for long and, after taking in the splendour of the setting sun, they went below to take their seats in the dining saloon. During the meal, the conversation came round to the noticeable drop in temperature during the day and the possible presence of icebergs in the area. Several people were hoping they might see one before the voyage was over. Although it was too dark that evening, they hoped they might catch sight of one the following day.

At 5.45 p.m., the freighter *Californian* spotted a huge ice field in the same position that had been reported earlier in the day.

After dinner that evening, the Browns attended their second Sunday service in the second-class lounge, this time conducted by Rev. Carter. Ironically, of the several hymns chosen for the service, the last one to be sung was the hymn *For Those in Peril on the Sea*.

At 9 p.m., the air temperature had fallen to just one degree above freezing. Travelling at 23 knots, the lookouts in the crow's-nest would have known all about the freezing temperatures, having been aloft in the open crow's-nest for the past hour. They had scant protection up there for their two-hour watch, apart from a canvass dodger of around chest height. There was virtually no room to move about in order to keep up their circulation.

After two hours on lookout, they would have been expected to be as vigilant as when they first went up the iron ladder inside of the mast at the start of their watch. It was at that time that the officer of the watch told the ship's carpenter to check the ship's supply of fresh water for any signs of freezing.

At 9.45, another ice report came in from the ship *Messaba*, again giving the same position for the massive ice field that lay ahead.

At 10.00, Elizabeth and Edith decided to retire to their cabin for the night, leaving Thomas to return to the smoking room after escorting the ladies below.

This was also the time for a change of lookouts, and before they were relieved, the two already in the crow's-nest had been told by the officer of the watch to keep a sharp lookout for ice and to pass it on to their relief's. At 10.30, the sea temperature had dropped to 31 degrees, and the air temperature had reached the freezing point. The British cargo ship *Rappahannock* signalled the *Titanic* by Morse lamp that she had just passed through a huge ice field. This was acknowledged by the officer of the watch and, after entering it in the log, he continued on the same course.

In the public rooms, passengers were enjoying their evening, playing cards or chatting amongst themselves over a drink or two as the ship's orchestra played popular tunes of the time. At 11.00, the freighter *Californian* attempted to transmit to the *Titanic* warnings of heavy ice, but was cut off by the *Titanic's* wireless operator due to his heavy workload of passengers' outgoing messages.

After an hour in the crow's-nest, Fred Fleet and Reginald Lee were beginning to feel the bitter cold. They couldn't wait for their relief at midnight. At 11.30, both men commented on a slight haze up ahead. Fog was always a possibility in those regions, and would shut down as quickly as first sighted. Just before 11.40, both men, staring intently ahead, quickly realised that it wasn't any fog bank looming out of the darkness. The huge haze drawing quickly closer had a definite fixed shape about it.

Five seconds, maybe more, passed before it finally revealed itself. A massive iceberg lay dead ahead and was approaching fast. Fleet grabbed the phone while Lee rang the bell three times as a warning of an object dead ahead, the correct lookout warning. The high-pitched whine from the phone in the wheelhouse made the junior officer jump before he rushed over to pick up the handset. 'What do you see?' asked the officer.

'Iceberg dead ahead!' shouted Fleet.

In the wheelhouse, the junior officer turned to First Officer Murdoch and repeated what he had just heard: 'Iceberg dead ahead, sir!'

Murdoch, straining his eyes to see out of the wheelhouse windows, shouted, 'Hard to port!' And then he shouted, 'Full astern on all engines!' and rushed out on to the starboard wing of the bridge. In the crow's-nest, Fleet and Lee watched in utter amazement as a huge iceberg loomed up out of the darkness, getting bigger every second. The *Titanic* appeared to be heading straight for it at ever-greater speed.

But slowly, ever so slowly, the *Titanic* began to turn to port.

The lookouts in the crow's-nest and the officers on the bridge watched with growing horror. It was becoming all too clear that she just wasn't going to make it.

CHAPTER EIGHT

TITANIC DAY SIX

At 1.30 a.m. on Monday, 15 April, most of the women and children destined for Lifeboat 14 were already in the boat. Elizabeth and Edith were ushered along by a crewmember saying, 'Come on ladies! Quick as you can!'

Elizabeth, extremely tearful by this time, turned her head around and shouted at Thomas, 'Get into another boat, Tom!' She implored him to go around to the other side of the boat deck to find a boat there. Almost falling as she was helped into the boat, she started to cry again as she sat alongside of Edith on one of the cross benches.

Seeing her mother in this state and looking back toward her father, Edith sat there with her hands in her lap as tears streamed down her face. Her father was making no effort to find another boat. He just stood there, gently puffing on his cigar and never taking his eyes off of them. Rev. Carter, who had just taken his wife, Lillian, to another lifeboat further along the sloping boat deck, had now returned to join him.

Suddenly, another rocket streaked into the night sky with a loud hiss. An explosion of sparks followed as it reached the top of its arc, lighting up the faces of the people who briefly looked up. Officer Lowe shouted to the crew on deck, 'Stand by to lower away!'

At that precise moment, several men surged forward in an effort to get into the hanging lifeboat, and three shots rang out in quick succession. Officer Lowe had fired his pistol above the advancing men's heads as a warning. Lowering his pistol, Officer Lowe shouted to the men, who had been halted by the gunshots. 'Try that again and it won't be warning shots I shall be firing, but shots aimed at anyone trying to get into this boat!' Pointing his pistol at the group, he shouted, 'Back off now!' With that, they backed away from the hanging lifeboat.

'Lower away together!' shouted Lowe. The crew on deck acknowledged his command with a wave and started to ease the falls around the bitts. Slowly and in jerky movements, Lifeboat 14 began to descend to the black, icy waters below. Officer Lowe must have thought about how the full boat, along with the davits, would stand up to the jerky lowering process, doubting if the gear had been tested to its fullest capacity. He would have realised that there was little he could do about that, and the sooner they reach the water, the better.

Looking up toward Thomas, Elizabeth shouted again to her husband to start looking for another lifeboat, but he remained standing in the same place, never taking his eyes off of them.

Edith joined in, crying out in desperation, 'Do what mother says! Find a boat, Father!' Tears were streaming down her face as Thomas gave them both a little wave and blew a kiss. She knew full well that the situation was hopeless for the men being left behind. Edith never forgot the sadness on her father's face, a sadness she had never seen before.

As the boat continued its jerky descent down the ship's side, Thomas, almost out of sight now, stepped forward and shouted down to both women, 'I'll see you in New York!'

Those were the last words they would ever hear from him. As their boat continued down the ship's side, Edith could see, through the lighted portholes, that some people were still in their cabins, grabbing what bits and pieces they could. The lights from some portholes that were completely submerged could be seen shining up through the icy water, giving the whole scene an extraordinary and unnatural effervescence

Just before reaching the water, one end of the lifeboat stopped as the other end continued to descend. Officer Lowe knew what the problem was; he shouted as hard as he could to the men up on deck to clear the falls and stop one end lowering. Amid the din, the poor lighting from above, and the inability to be heard back up on deck, it became futile. The falls had jammed around the bitts on deck, and with the weight of the boat and its occupants, it would be impossible to free it. As the boat was almost touching the water, there was only one solution, and that was to cut the falls.

'Get your knife out and cut the bloody falls!' shouted Lowe to the able seaman sitting in the bow of the boat. The fault had stopped that end from lowering any further.

With a few slices of the seaman's knife, the lines parted and the boat crashed into the sea, splashing the occupants and shipping a great deal of icy water. Passengers fell about at the impact, screaming and shouting and fearing they would all be dumped in the sea. There was another shout; water was spouting up from the bottom of the boat, where the impact with the water had forced out the plug. With some luck, the bung was quickly replaced, but not before several inches of water had pooled in the bottom of the boat. Plugs were usually chained adjacent to the plughole and could be easily found, but no doubt things were difficult in a cramped lifeboat full of women and children falling over each other.

Elizabeth and Edith looked down at their feet. Until the water was bailed out, the best part of their footwear was going to be under water. Edith always remembered the beautiful leather calf-length, button-up boots with the pointed toes that her father had bought them in London, but now they were ruined.

Once the boat had settled in the water, the hooks at each end were released and cleared, and the boat was pushed away from the ship's side with oars. It was vital to get away from the ship as soon as possible for safety reasons. Some passengers still on deck could be in a state of near panic. They could throw over the side anything that floated, preparing to take their chances in the icy water. Deck chairs and other wooden fittings falling into loaded lifeboats could cause no end of injuries, or even death, and any good coxswain in a boat that night would have cleared the vessel as soon as possible.

The correct abandon-ship procedure would include plans for the safety of the lifeboats and their occupants. Once away, they were to find other boats and tether themselves to each other, and this is what Officer Lowe did. This procedure would ensure that there was an even distribution of passengers between all boats. It also made for easy recognition when search vessels finally arrived on the scene.

Elizabeth raised her head and looked back. She tried to fix her gaze on the place on the boat deck where she had last seen her beloved Thomas, but due to the poor light it was practically impossible to make out where he might be at that time. Edith, as though reading her thoughts, tried to comfort her mother by saying that he had probably gone to the other side of the ship and had most likely found another boat.

'Oh, God, I hope so!' Elizabeth said. 'But he never even had a lifejacket on!' Again she broke down, with Edith doing her best to comfort her as her own tears fell easily down her cheeks.

Another distress rocket streaked up from the *Titanic's* bridge, arcing over and lighting up the immediate vicinity with its starburst. As soon as Officer Lowe decided they were far enough away from the ship, he ordered the rowers to, 'Rest oars!' They stopped rowing and leaned forward on their oars, looking back at the slowly dying ship, her bows almost completely submerged. They hardly believed what they were witnessing. In the lifeboats, there was a sob or a cough now and then as they continued to look back at the nightmare unfolding before their very eyes. It must have been a different scene on board the ship; shouts, screams, and banging, crashing noises came across the still water, growing louder and longer as the minutes ticked by.

Puffs of vapour marked the breaths of the lifeboats' occupants; the night air was icy cold. Edith had turned her head away to comfort her mother, but now she looked back as the grating, crashing, and creaking noises grew louder. They were the sounds of twisted, tortured metal and woodwork.

Despite those devastating sounds from across the water, music could still be heard now and then, coming from somewhere up on the boat deck. The ship's deck lights still shone down on the water, and lights could still be seen from many portholes as the stern of the *Titanic* continued to rise slowly out of the water. Masses of people could be seen making their way along the decks toward the stern, as there were now no more lifeboats left on the ship. With no boats or life-saving gear, the only option left open to them was to hang on to their lives to the bitter end by getting to the highest part of the ship and hoping that some miracle might save them from the icy death that was fast approaching.

As the lifeboats circled the stricken liner at a safe distance, the occupants could see that the forward section of the ship had now completely disappeared below the sea. There were thunderous noises coming from deep within the hull, followed by screeches, screams, and shouts that grew louder across the still water. The crashing of broken glass and the booming noises of bulkheads giving way were followed by tremendous thuds as huge sections of machinery crashed through the ship toward the submerged end.

Edith and her mother watched and listened in horror. They put their hands over their ears to block out the sounds of human suffering, but those noises were to haunt Edith for the rest of her life.

Suddenly, there was a shout from one of the boat's crew. 'The funnel is falling over!'

With that, there was a gasp from the boats as the foremost funnel appeared to teeter over before the wire stays snapped. It crashed into the sea amid clouds of steam, smoke and a shower of sparks.

At this time, people were seen to be jumping into the sea as the stern continued to rise up. Then it appeared to settle back slightly, before finally following the forward end down into the depths of the icy Atlantic. The screams and cries for help were drowned out briefly as huge underwater explosions erupted, sending towering spumes to the surface as the flagstaff at the *Titanic's* very stern finally disappeared below the sea.

CHAPTER NINE

CARPATHIA

The gurgling and bubbling noises began to abate as the surface of the water began to settle, leaving a slight mist where the *Titanic* had finally disappeared just a few moments ago. 'Make way together!' shouted Lowe.

Once more, hundreds of cries for help could be heard from people in the water. They were scattered over a wide area. Lifeboat 14 returned to an area of concentrated cries and moans and managed to pull four people out of the water. One of them died soon after; another appeared to be in a very bad way but was quickly wrapped in a blanket in an attempt to keep him warm.

Edith and her mother remained cuddled together, looking down once in a while at the water in the bottom of the boat. Their sodden boots had left them with no feeling in their feet.

That night, the lifeboats drifted around the wreck site, an area of almost three square miles. Everyone suffered from the effects of the extreme cold. As the early hours of the morning approached, there was silence across the water, broken only by a cough now and then, a whimper from a child, and the water gently lapping the planking around the sides of the boat. The cold had had its searching effects on all of them as they waited for daybreak and possible rescue. As dawn broke several hours later, the scene before them was one of enormous tragedy. There were bodies everywhere, some with life jackets on, floating silently in an upright position. Among the corpses were many women and children, frozen to death and still clinging to each other as they drifted amongst the ice. As daylight approached, it could be seen that they were in the middle of a vast ice field with several small icebergs scattered around in a wide area. Some of the bodies were those of the crew; some wore only vests and clung to wooden gratings; others were still in their working kit, clinging on to deck chairs tied together. All had frozen to death from the intense cold.

At 6 a.m., a shout from one of the boat's crew roused many of the occupants of the lifeboats. 'I can see a steamer's lights!' the man shouted.

Officer Lowe, in the stern of the boat, shouted back, 'Where do you see it?'

Pointing ahead of them, the seaman shouted, 'You can see her mast-head light!'

Lowe, now standing up on a seat in the stern of the boat, exclaimed, 'By Christ, you're right! It's the *Carpathia*!'

To many in the boats, it appeared that the ship was hardly moving at all.

The *Carpathia's* master, Captain Rostron, had a great deal of responsibility on his hands at this time. Picking his way through the ice field that had just sunk the *Titanic*, he had 700 of his own passengers to look out for, plus his own crew and ship.

Once Captain Rostron was satisfied that his ship was in a good position, away from ice and close to most lifeboats, he stopped his engines and made preparations to pick up survivors. The shell doors in the side of the ship were no more than twelve to fifteen feet above the waterline; the *Carpathia* was only a quarter of the size of the *Titanic*, making the climb and lift on board a short one.

Those who could climb the Jacob's ladder did so. The crew lifted some of the children on board in small mailbags; other children and women were lifted on board by boatswain's chair. Stewards and stewardesses were there to assist them on board, and they brought hot soup, brandy, and bread rolls as survivors were brought alongside from other boats and settled down in the lounges on board.

Edith and her mother had great difficulty in walking once on board the *Carpathia* as they waited for the circulation to slowly return to their legs and feet. The crew on board the *Carpathia* had been well briefed on what to expect during their voyage to the wreck site and had organised bedding and clothing for those coming on board. The passengers, on the *Carpathia* for a Mediterranean cruise, would never have realised just what sort of mercy mission they were going to get involved in.

Many, including Edith and her mother, would never forget their humanitarian response in helping survivors by offering clothing and, in some cases, their cabins.

As the circulation returned slowly, they began talking to other survivors about their ordeals over the past eight hours. Their stories were similar, with many women fearing for the safety of their men-folk.

Their conversations were interrupted every time another boat came alongside, with everyone rushing to the ship's side to see if any of their loved ones had been saved. Elizabeth and her daughter followed them to the ship's rail in the hope that Thomas might be one of the few men who had been rescued, but each time, the boats were loaded with women and children and one or two crew. As the last boats slowly came alongside, it was beginning to look as though there were going to be many widows when they finally arrived in New York. Of all the women rescued that morning, only four were found to still have husbands, but there was hope that more would be found in hospitals in New York. Once all the boats were cleared, they were hoisted on board by the ship's derricks and stowed for delivery to the White Star wharf in New York.

As time went by, it was becoming obvious to everyone that no more survivors would be found. Later, a count was taken by the senior purser and officers. The count revealed a tragedy of enormous proportions, a tragedy unmatched in maritime history. Of the estimated 2,225 persons on board the *Titanic* just twelve hours ago, there were now only 705 survivors accounted for. The only other ship in the area was the *Californian*, which had been stopped all night in the ice field. She had now arrived on the scene alongside of the *Carpathia*, far too late to be of any real help, but offered to transfer some of the passengers off of the *Carpathia*. Captain Rostron had refused, realising that to put some of the traumatised survivors back into a lifeboat to transfer them across to the other ship was not an option. He suggested that the *Californian* remain in the area and continue to search for any survivors whilst he headed for New York. After agreeing on this course of action with Captain Lord of the *Californian,* the *Carpathia* slowly altered course and began to navigate her way out of the ice field. It took several hours for the ship to clear the ice before nightfall, but the captain had no inclination to spend a night in that area.

Edith and her mother, having been on deck for long periods of time in the hope of finding Thomas, were now feeling cold again. They made for one of the lounges for some well-earned sleep, if sleep was possible. As the *Carpathia* steamed for New York, Elizabeth and Edith began to wonder what the future now held for them. They both agreed that they shouldn't give up hope until they had arrived in New York and a final check of the survivors was carried out. There were rumours going around that there was a possibility that other ships in the area had heard the distress calls and had picked up survivors, but their wireless equipment wasn't up to the job of reporting this news. It had been suggested that many old ships out there might well have had trouble transmitting (radio communications were still in the early stages of development).

Elizabeth knew that any belief in those rumours was clutching at straws, but it was feasible, and it did give them hope until their arrival in America. During their voyage to New York, both women cried every time they spoke of Thomas not being rescued. But it was better not to think the worst.

The day before their arrival in New York, Edith and her mother were feeling greatly improved after their experiences over the last few days. Like her mother had said, it would all come out once they arrived in New York, and perhaps her father would be there on the wharf, waiting for them. This train of thought made Edith feel better, and she was going to stick with it until she knew differently.

Elizabeth, on the other hand, knew that it would take something just short of a miracle to bring her dearest Tom back to her. And she knew she would have to prepare her daughter for the worst fairly soon. Edith had idolised her father all her life, and he in turn had spoiled her since the death of her younger sister, Dorothy, back in 1908.

Sitting in the lounge after lunch on the final day on board the *Carpathia,* Elizabeth explained to her daughter how their financial situation would be affected if Thomas had drowned. She went on to say that all their money to start up the new business in Seattle would have been in Thomas's Gladstone bag, which had been locked away securely in the purser's office.

'That being the case,' she said, 'it might now be at the bottom of the ocean. Whatever the outcome in New York, the plans we had for Seattle just don't apply anymore.'

Edith realised just how much her mother was now confiding in her. As a result, she was beginning to feel more grown-up and responsible.

Her mother said, 'We will have to continue on to Seattle, as we just don't know anyone else in America. And besides, your Aunt Josephine would be expecting that.'

The stark realisation of their predicament finally came to Edith when her mother said, 'What I'm trying to say to you, my dear, is that we no longer have any visible means of support or any money to speak of.'

Edith had never had to think about money before. She knew what her mother was saying, but she didn't fully understand at that time just what it might mean for her future. The only thing that really mattered to her was if she would ever see her father again. After giving their state of affairs further thought, Edith asked her mother if she thought her father would stay in America after losing all that money.

Sadly, her mother replied, 'I wouldn't think so, my dear.'

CHAPTER TEN

NEW YORK

On a bleak Thursday night at 8 p.m. on 18 April 1912, the *Carpathia* slowly steamed up the Hudson River, heading for the White Star berth. She was accompanied by a flotilla of small craft and tugboats crammed full of sightseers and photographers, many of them shouting through loud hailers to those on board the *Carpathia*. Berthing briefly at the wharf where the *Titanic* would have berthed, she unloaded all that was left of her lifeboats, all showing the name *Titanic* on their bows. The *Carpathia* then moved upstream several berths to the usual Cunard Line berth and, with the help of a tugboat, gently moored up alongside. This, then, was the end of a journey on which so many with hope in their hearts had perished. Those who survived had lived through one of the greatest tragedies in maritime history.

The scene that greeted them on the dockside was overwhelming, and it was a sight that Edith and her mother would never forget. It looked as though the whole of New York had braved the foul weather to come down to the wharves to witness the arrival of the *Titanic* survivors. As the gangways were placed in position, there were shouts from the quayside to those on board, leaning on the ship's rail. It was a never-ending barrage of questions. 'Did you see many dead bodies in the water?' 'Have you lost anyone?' 'Do you need any money?' And so it went on.

Not surprisingly, the class system still applied, and the first-class survivors were the first off, amid a blaze of flash bulbs and dozens of reporters surging forward to the bottom of the gangway. They were soon protected by shore personnel and whisked away in taxis or their own transport. Elizabeth and Edith soon followed as the second-class passengers were given instructions to go ashore. Once on the dockside, there was pushing and shoving, making it impossible to move forward at times, until several burly New York policemen cleared a path for them. When they had slowly made their way into the cargo shed, they were led to a group of offices at one end. It had been decided that all single women would be under the care of the Women's Junior League of New York. The women would remain under their care until other suitable arrangements could be made and relatives could be contacted. The generosity shown by the Americans was something Edith never forgot.

From a newspaper report in *The Seattle Daily Times, April 16, 1912.*

TERRIBLE DISASTERS MARK WINTER SEASON.

The prevalence of icebergs on the Grand Banks this season is due to the exceptional severity of the recent winter, which is perhaps the worst in the history of Newfoundland and Labrador. From mid-December up to the present time intense frost and incessant storms have prevailed. These conditions caused the ice forming in every harbour along Labrador and Northern Newfoundland to become unusually thick, and as the severe winds tore the masses from the coast, these immense crystal mountains were flung widespread over the ocean.

They were carried south by the current from the polar region, which, meeting the Gulf Stream caused constant fogs which so greatly menaced shipping.

Again, there had been an extremely mild winter in the Arctic, owing to which, ice from the ice cap and glaciers had broken away in phenomenal quantities and official reports say that never before or since has there been known to be such quantities of icebergs, growlers, field ice and float ice, stretching down the Labrador current. 'In my fifteen years experience on the Atlantic, I had certainly never seen anything like it' (C.H.Lightoller, second officer, R.M.S. Titanic.)

Lightoller's comments on the 'mild' 1912 winter weather have often been repeated as facts by authors and screenwriters. The spring of 1912 was indeed mild. However, the preceding winter was, by all accounts, off the charts! The article went on to say:

One wonders how White Star folks could have been so blissfully unaware of these conditions, since many were employed at the New York office, and others had spent time in the city prior to their return to England for the Titanic's April departure.

The full story of the sinking of the *Titanic* was becoming clear, despite the many false reports from the world's news agencies. People became angry when they read that more third-class children had died than men from the first class. Of the third class, 535 men, women, and children were lost, and only 175 were saved. In the second class, 165 passengers were lost, and 200 were saved. In the first class, 128 were lost, and 200 were saved. Out of a crew of almost 900, only 215 were saved.

Of the twenty-three stewardesses on board, three drowned after giving up their places in the boats for women and children. All seven members of the ship's orchestra had lost their lives, playing music for as long as it was possible to do so. Every mail sorter had died, trying to save sacks of mail and packages to the bitter end. All the bellboys had drowned; they had not been allowed into the boats because they were considered crew, despite some of them being as young as 14. All the engineers had perished in their final attempts to keep the utilities running and the ship afloat for as long as possible.

The headlines in most newspapers made grim reading. A total of 1,520 souls had lost their lives in the freezing waters of the North Atlantic.

On arrival at the hostel, Edith and her mother had a hot meal and a bath and finally retired for the night, quite exhausted by the day's events. The next day, they were taken shopping. They returned with more clothes than they would ever need, as the Americans went out of their way to make sure they would want for nothing.

After the lengthy shopping spree, they were taken around to several hospitals in New York to check for survivors, but all to no avail. They knew in their hearts that they would never see Thomas again.

On returning to the hostel, Elizabeth said to her daughter, 'It's just you and me now, Edith.'

From a newspaper report in *The Seattle Daily Times, April 18, 1912*

SEATTLE RELATIVES WAITING FOR NEWS

Edward Acton whose wife is a sister of Mrs. T.W.S. Brown expects a relayed message from two of the Titanic's survivors from Cape Town, South Africa to their Seattle relatives hourly. She, with her husband and daughter, were on their way to Seattle, passengers on the ill-fated leviathan. The Actons so far have only had press reports as to the fate of their relatives. The meagre information these contained is that a T.W.S. Brown is on the Carpathia. The hope the Actons are clinging to be in the hasty preparation of the list was that Mrs Brown was overlooked. It is also possible the she and both her husband were saved. Yesterday Mr Acton who is a teller in The Northern Bank and Trust Company sent a message direct to T.W.S Brown, care of the Carpathia at sea beseeching the survivors immediately to send by wireless correct or confirmation of the newspaper report.

After the *Carpathia's* arrival in New York, Senator William Alden Smith lost no time in setting up an enquiry. The Americans knew that the British would also hold an enquiry as soon all the crew had returned to England. It was therefore considered essential to hold an enquiry before those crewmembers returned to England, whilst the events of that night were still fresh in people's minds.

As the *Carpathia* had steamed toward New York, White Star had chartered two vessels out of Halifax, Nova Scotia, to search the area for bodies. One of the vessels, the *Mackay Bennet*, had picked up over 300 bodies, putting on ice those that had been identified and burying the remaining 112 at sea. Many of the corpses were clad in heavy clothing and life jackets, but the sea temperature had been two degrees below freezing and the main cause of death. The other ship chartered for this gruesome task was the *Minia*, which continued to search for another week after the *Mackay Bennet* had returned to Halifax. By the first week in May, the weather had deteriorated; there were strong winds and heavy rain. As a result, fewer bodies were found. A few weeks later, the search was called off. Some two weeks after that, another body was found and buried at sea by a passing steamer.

Another newspaper item with several sub headings to emphasise the tragedy by *The Seattle Daily Times, April 19, 1912*.

RELATIVES OF SEATTLE PEOPLE AMONG THOSE WHO DIED ON TITANIC.

Among thousands here who mourn tragedy of North Atlantic are some whose hearts are breaking.
Reunion of sisters marred by shipwreck

Mr. And Mrs. T.W.S. Brown and daughter who were on way here to visit relatives were on lost liner.

Among the many thousands in Seattle who are today joining in the nation's mourning for the loss of those brave ones who went down on board the Titanic there are few whose hearts are breaking, for they had loved ones on the lost ship.
Hope for most of them is buried as deep as the ill-fated ship.
One Seattle woman learned that her sister was among those who escaped, though her name was not in the first list of survivors, only to learn at the same time that the husband of the supposed victim had gone down with the ocean liner.

The US enquiry got underway without delay, and some of the able seamen were questioned at the start of the proceedings. Bruce Ismay, the managing director of White Star Line, was called to give evidence. He was questioned about his role whilst on board the *Titanic*, and he claimed repeatedly that he was no more than a passenger. He maintained that Captain Smith was always in command of his ship, and Senator Alden Smith found it difficult to get him to deviate from that theme during questioning.

The lookouts were questioned about their instructions to watch for ice, and they replied that they had done just that. They were also questioned about the lack of binoculars. They said they might have seen the iceberg had a pair been available, but it was doubtful if they would have seen it any sooner than with the naked eye. They also confirmed that the bridge had responded instantly once they had received the report from the crow's-nest.

During their stay at the Women's Junior League in New York, Elizabeth sent a cable to her sister in Seattle, letting Josephine know they were safe, but that Thomas was feared drowned. She finished off by saying they would be taking an interstate train to Seattle within a week.

The newspapers were full of the disaster, and Elizabeth and Edith scanned them daily in the hope they might find Thomas's body, if nothing else. It was beginning to look pointless to hope for any missing passengers to turn up, and so Elizabeth decided to make arrangements for their journey to Seattle. Elizabeth told her daughter about their money situation. She said that whenever they had travelled, they always had gold sovereigns with them. These were carried in a money belt around her father's waist and were also sewn into the seams of some of his waistcoats. Robbery had always been of great concern to them both, and by carrying the money in this fashion, they had felt safer.

Edith showed great interest in what her mother was saying. She was even more surprised when she learned that both of their grey, ankle-length coats with the velvet cuffs and collars had also had some sovereign's sewn in around the hems. Edith asked if this was all the money they had left in the world. Her mother said that her father had left some shares in the wine and brandy companies back in South Africa, but she didn't know how much they were worth.

The US enquiry moved to Washington, where other important witnesses appeared, including Captain Lord of the *Californian*. There was criticism regarding the *Californian's* failure to investigate further the rockets sighted whilst they were stationary in the ice field the night of 15 April. The *Californian's* officers had tried a Morse lamp, had seen the rockets, and had decided after 2 a.m. that the ship had steamed away.

The enquiry concluded that the *Californian* had been in a position to come to the aid of the sinking *Titanic* and should have made a greater effort to investigate the rockets they sighted. The findings of the enquiry are a matter of controversy to this very day. Senator Smith, in winding up his findings, labelled those responsible for the safety of the *Titanic* as negligent and recommended sweeping changes for safety at sea.

During Elizabeth and Edith's stay in New York, the press hounded them everywhere they went. Elizabeth knew only too well that it was because of the press that so many people came forward to help them, and for that, they would be forever grateful. The press could be overwhelming at times, stopping them in the street and forever asking the same questions. Both women became expert with ready answers. At other times, they would duck into a ladies' lavatory to get away from the throng and collect their thoughts.

It was decided that they would travel by train to Seattle at the end of the week. They had no idea how far it was, but had been advised by some well-wishers that the journey could take up to five days. They did their final shopping; again, many people insisted on paying for everything and went out of their way to help in any way they could. Their last day in New York was one of sadness, feeling in a strange sort of way that they were finally laying Thomas to rest. He had been a wonderful father and husband. There was also a bit of sadness at leaving behind the many kind people who had, in such a short time, become their friends. They would never be able to thank them enough, and they would never forget the kindness they had shown them.

On arrival at New York's Grand Central Station, several well-wishers and the inevitable press greeted Elizabeth and her daughter. They were to journey through ten states, a journey totalling some 2,000 miles. Neither looked forward to it, but there was no alternative.

The huge locomotive, with its great lantern situated in front of its bell-shaped chimney and cow catchers in front of its bogey wheels, began to slowly pull out of the station. There were shouts of 'good luck' from those left behind on the platform as they started on their great journey west. As the train cleared the station and gathered speed, they settled back in their seats for the first leg of their journey. On their arrival in Cleveland, quite surprisingly, they were again met by reporters.

Both women, quite expert with interviews now, told them what they wanted to hear and dismissed them with relative ease. The next leg of their journey took them to Chicago. They travelled along the banks of Lake Erie, with its river valleys and steep, forested hills, continuing through the state of Indiana, bordering Lake Michigan. With summer approaching, the scenery was quite spectacular at times. Edith always maintained that this was some of the best scenery she had ever seen. After a lengthy stop in Chicago and a change of trains, they were bound for Minneapolis. This turned out to be a long haul of ten hours or more, passing through the state of Illinois, with its rich farmlands reaching from Lake Michigan to the Mississippi River.

Those long hours on the train were made bearable by looking out the windows at the rolling plains, hills, and valleys of the beautiful state of Illinois. After the long journey from Chicago, Edith and her mother were relieved when the train finally pulled into St Paul, known as the twin city to Minneapolis. Situated on the banks of the Mississippi, it was a fast-growing frontier town with wide-open spaces and lakes. After this stop, they continued on their journey through Minnesota, which bordered Canada and Lake Superior, the largest freshwater lake in the world. Their train traversed the many forests of the upper Midwest and entered North Dakota, famous for its scenery and spectacular views. Although both women were tired and wanted the long journey to end, they remained spellbound by the wonderful scenery.

The train stopped at Fargo, the biggest town in the state, before setting off again for Billings, Montana, on the eastern fringe of the Rocky Mountains. Famous for Custer's Last Stand, the state had many canyons and rough riding country. On arrival at Billings, they had another lengthy stay before going on to Spokane. Setting off once again, they travelled through the rest of Montana, well known as one of America's most scenic states. This was a state of vast areas of wilderness, great ranches, and cattle drives. They saw much wildlife including deer, elk, and antelope. Taking in the scenery, Edith and her mother had some time to take their minds off of recent events. It was a welcome, if temporary, relief.

As their train wound its way around the spectacular Rocky

Mountains, Edith thought about Seattle. It no longer gave her the excitement she had first felt. This was understandable, with the loss of her father and their future now in ruins.

They later crossed the state of Idaho and entered Washington State. They felt relief on arriving in Spokane, their last stop before Seattle. From here, Elizabeth sent a cable to her sister Josephine to let her know their expected time of arrival.

On arrival in the Seattle train station, reporters once again confronted them. The newspapers were still full of stories about the *Titanic*, and both women were inundated with a barrage of questions from reporters. Josephine and her husband, Ed Acton, arrived on the scene and helped them get away from the surging crowds. Once away from the station, Elizabeth broke down. Many of the questions had been about the death of her husband and other insensitive topics. The long train journey had been a distraction from their tragedy, allowing them to take in the beautiful, refreshing scenery as it swept past their carriage windows day after day. To be confronted by all those reporters on their arrival had just been too much after such a long journey.

Josephine and her husband did their best, organising a room for them, making life as comfortable as possible, and giving both women some peace and quiet for several days.

Once the were feeling more up to it, they were able to give some lengthy interviews; parts of these are quoted below.

From the *Seattle (Wa) Post- Intelligencer, April 26, 1912.*

Woman survivor of Titanic joins her sister here.

Mrs. T.W.S. Brown of Cape Town, South Africa, is in Seattle at the home of her sister, Mrs. Edward Acton. With her is her daughter, Edith, sixteen years of age. Husband and father turned his back on lifeboat 14 when it was lowered from Titanic's boat deck, and so they parted.

'Bad luck pursued Titanic from the start' said Mrs. Brown. 'My husband had a strange premonition at Southampton. As we entered the big gates leading to the pier, he turned back suddenly and his face went white.'

'What is it?' I asked.

'Oh nothing,' he said. 'Later he told me something was going to happen. If we had heeded that warning and turned back then, we might have been together now.

'The first day at sea passengers heard that the Titanic was afire. The officers denied it, but I was told on good authority that there was a fire in one of the coalbunkers, and a special crew of men were kept at work day and night to keep it under control. I believe this to be true. We met a gentleman whom I believe to be Mr. Harbeck of Seattle. I did not hear his name clearly, but he was from Seattle and said he was from show business there. He talked often to my husband and gave him his card. He was very pleasant and gave us much valuable information about Seattle. We went to our berths several hours before the accident Sunday night.

'I was awakened by a shock. It seemed violent to me. I feared at once that there had been an accident. The passengers had seen reports about icebergs on the ship's bulletins and of course there was much talk about them among us, just as we discussed the speed the ship was making and speculated as to when we should reach New York.

'My first thought was we have struck an iceberg. I put some clothes on and told my daughter to dress. My husband did not think the situation was dangerous but I urged him to go on deck and find out what had happened.

'I did not think to dress very warmly, but put on my best clothes that I had been wearing on Sunday. I had low slippers on. Presently my husband came back to me. He looked very serious. "Get on these cork jackets," he said. He then helped Edith and me into life jackets. He linked his arm into mine and led me up to the boat deck. He said that women and children were being put into lifeboats and that we had struck a berg.

'I saw what seemed to be tons of ice on the forward deck. The ship seemed to have crashed far into the berg. "Now keep up as best you can and be saved," said my husband.

There was great excitement on the deck. He led us to lifeboat 14. The men were all standing back from the boat, but some of the women were struggling to get in. My daughter and I stepped in. My husband turned away without a word. I thought he would follow us into the boat. Some of the foreign steerage passenger men were struggling to get into the boat. I heard an officer threaten to shoot them if they came near.

'The boat was crowded mostly with women. I afterwards found there *were sixty persons in it. We stood or sat wherever we could in a thick crowd. They began to lower the boat over the side. It seemed a terrible distance.*

'*Ours was the second boat off. As it lay in the water alongside of Titanic, a foreign steerage passenger suddenly dived from way up on the boat deck right into our boat. We were afraid someone would be struck and killed. The man did not seem to be hurt. Some of the men threatened to kill anybody else that tried that. We pushed off.*

'*The men in the boat seemed to be mostly members of the crew. It was terribly cold. Most of the women seemed to be lightly clad or half clad. I stood almost knee deep in water that had gotten into the bottom of the boat.*

'*We pulled a short way from the wreck. We could see the Titanic quite plainly. As she began to sink at the bow, we could see the men climb and run to the upper parts of her. There they stood in groups quite silent. Some seemed to have their arms folded.*

'*As the Titanic went down by the head there seemed to be an explosion. Then we heard screams and saw people jumping. After the ship went down, we drifted about. We saw a man swimming. He had a baby in one arm. He came up to our boat and somebody took the baby from him and gave it to the women to care for. Then the man climbed in. I do not know who he was.*

'*We were nine hours in the lifeboat before the Carpathia came up to us. We were treated as well as one could expect on the Carpathia. There was no place for us to sleep so we laid down in passageways or wherever we could spread a mattress.*

'*When we reached New York the passengers were divided into groups and cared for by various organisations. I had some money so I could buy clothes but many women did not and I divided up with them.*'

The newspaper went on to say that Mrs Brown had nothing but praise for the officers of the *Titanic*. She declared they did their very best. They also mentioned her telegraphing her sister, Mrs Acton, from New York, and went on to say that the sisters were reunited last night at the King Street station. They added that the scene was touching; Mrs Brown and her daughter still showed the effects from exposure and were prostrated by grief. As in other survivor interviews, there are many inaccuracies in the above newspaper report. The press report concluded that Mrs Brown and her daughter were still showing the effects of exposure and grief, which was probably a good reason for such inaccuracies.

In Washington, the Senate enquiry into the sinking of the *Titanic* was drawing to a close. Most of the important witnesses had testified. One of those was Fifth Officer Lowe of Lifeboat 14, who made a statement to confirm that the use of his pistol was only for warning men away from the boat. His priority was to get as many women and children into the boat as possible, and to prevent the boat from becoming swamped by too many people. He maintained that there was no truth in the allegation that he had fired his pistol to prevent emigrants from getting into the boat, while other classes were given priority.

At the same time, another interview by the same newspaper the, *Seattle (Wa) Daily Times,* ran Edith's account.

Girl survivor says lifeboats were not all accounted for.

Miss Brown's Story

We had retired early for the evening of the terrible disaster, said *Miss Brown.*
I had been asleep for some time when I heard a crash and a slight jar. I awakened my mother and she called my father who was in a separate compartment. He went on deck and soon returned saying that the boat had struck an iceberg, but there was no danger. We then went back to bed.
A few minutes later my father returned and said to dress and that there was some danger. When he spoke this time he acted queerly and did not look either my mother or myself in the face when he told us. We dressed hurriedly and I put on some extra warm garments.
Some men attempted to get into the boat and the officer who was in charge, drew his revolver and shot it into the air and said that he would kill anyone that tried to jump in. This I think accounts for some of the stories about men being killed for trying to get into the boat. However, just as they started to lower our boat, a foreigner, whose nationality I could not

determine, leapt into it and it was too late to make him go back.

Some women refused to leave their husbands or escorts and it became necessary while loading our boat, in which there were about fifty, to force some of then to get in. With the exception of the man who jumped in and the officer and four firemen who manned the boat, I do not recall that there were other men in the boat. I think they were all women and children.

There was but little confusion attending the loading of the boats. With rare exception the men stood back or assisted the women and did everything possible to avert a panic. This I judge from the feeling of those of who I was in the lifeboat. I do not believe from their attitude and the things that they said that there was anyone among them who believed the Titanic would sink when we left her.

It would be almost impossible to one aboard to believe she could sink. She was so big and palatial that one could never forget that we were on the sea and the idea that anything so monstrous could be hurled to the bottom of the ocean was quite incomprehensible.

Like her mother's, this report from Edith has several inaccuracies. In this case, it could have been because of her age, what she had gone through as a young girl, and, of course, the pressure from the media to get these interviews into print. As a family, we always believed what our mother told us over the years. She had no reason to tell us anything other than the truth as she remembered it.

One point of interest is that she always maintained that the last words her father said to them both were, and I quote, 'I'll see you in New York, my dears.' It doesn't appear in either interview, but she wouldn't have forgotten that, as she loved her father dearly.

The following is a copy from the *Cape Town Argus, April 23, 1912,* reporting on the death of T.W.S. Brown.

The Titanic Disaster
Drowning of T.W.S. Brown (formerly of the Masonic Hotel)

We learn from Mr. J.H.P. Bosman, Napier St, Worcester, that he had received an intimation from his son, Mr. W. Bosman, Cape Town, that he had on Tuesday a cable from America announcing that his wife's father,

Mr. T.W.S. Brown, was one of the passengers who went down on the ill-fated Titanic and was drowned. Mr. Brown's wife and youngest daughter, who were accompanying him, were saved in the boats. We gather from further inquiries that Mr. Brown sailed from Cape Town fully two months ago with his wife and daughter, and had resided in London for a time pending the sailing of the Titanic, as they had made up their minds to cross over to America in the magnificent new ship, with disastrous results.

Mr. John Bosman (mayor) has favoured us with other interesting particulars of the deceased gentleman with whom he had been in touch, more or less, since his departure some ten years ago. Mr. Thomas William Solomon Brown had been associated with hotels in South Africa prior to acquiring the Masonic Hotel, Worcester, in the ownership of, which he remained for about eight years. He raised and well maintained the reputation of the hotel and during the war (Boer) made it a lucrative business. He made a good name for himself, as a reliable man whose word was his bond, and whose character was above reproach. He never sought public position or notoriety, but with his wife and daughters devoted his whole attention to his private affairs. Eventually he disposed of his hotel to Mr. J. Carrol for twelve thousand pounds and retired with his family to the suburbs of Cape Town. His investments were mostly in cottage property in Muisenberg, Kalk Bay and other places, and he was more or less interested in hotels in Johannesburg and Bloemfontein.

Mr. Brown's first wife had predeceased him, and he had married again before coming to Worcester. The first family comprised of two sons and two daughters, one of the latter, marrying Mr. Bosman of Cape Town whilst they were resident in Worcester. Mr. Brown had only one surviving daughter by his second wife, the younger having died at the age of eight from diphtheria, and of who was accompanying him to the United States at the time of his death. Just before departure from Cape Town, Mr. J.W. Bosman met him in Adderley Street, and, speaking of his intention to proceed with his wife and daughter to join relatives in America, said he had disposed of all his property about South Africa and only retained some shares in the Western Wine and Brandy Co. to remind him of Worcester and the people he had known there. He always entertained warm feelings towards them.

Mr. Brown was over 60 years of age. Nothing is known of the intentions of Mrs. Brown and daughter rescued from the Titanic, nor whether they were able to save any of their effects. The probability is that everything they were taking to America went down with the ship. News now anxiously awaited by mail.

After several weeks of living with Edward and Josephine, it was becoming clear that with Thomas gone, there wasn't any future for Elizabeth and her daughter in Seattle. There was the matter of tying up Thomas's estate back in South Africa, where he still had shares in wine and brandy companies. Besides, Elizabeth and her daughter were virtually penniless after using up what sovereigns they had left. The time had come for them to start planning their return trip to Cape Town. Although both women were dreading the long journey back across America and then the North Atlantic, there was no alternative.

Josephine's husband, Edward, had been busy organising their journey by rail and sea with the help of his colleagues at the bank. Once back in New York, they would stay for a few days before sailing for Liverpool. They would then travel to Southampton, and again, after a few days at a hotel, sail with Union Castle line to Cape Town. The whole journey would take some six weeks before they arrived back in South Africa.

They said their tearful goodbyes at the train station in Seattle and once again settled down for the very long journey ahead of them. On arrival in New York, Elizabeth told her daughter that she never wanted to set eyes on another train again for the rest of her life.

After a short stay in New York, they boarded their ship. This was to be a nervous time for both of them, knowing they would be travelling over the same course as that taken by the *Titanic*. Before sailing, Edith remembers asking the bedroom steward about ice. He replied that it wasn't a problem in the summer, and had she heard about the *Titanic*? Edith always remembered her mother's reply to the steward. 'Yes, we've heard about the *Titanic* and were unfortunate enough to have been on her at the time!' The steward, apologising several times over, made a quick exit from their cabin without further ado.

Their ship sailed from New York around noon, both women somewhat relieved to know that the threat of icebergs would not be of any concern on this voyage back to England. Edith remembered that on those first few days, the ship's siren sounded repeatedly as they went through one fog bank after another. She also remembered that her mother stayed below most of the time. Edith once again found the ship's library an interesting place to pass away the hours during the voyage. Edith ventured up on deck more on her own and began to talk more freely to other passengers, more so than she did on the *Titanic*. Edith would be 16 in October and was beginning to feel more like an adult, especially now that her mother was confiding in her more. On one occasion, an elderly couple asked her if she was the young girl who had been rescued from the *Titanic*. It left her a bit surprised at the way the news had travelled since talking to the bedroom steward.

The usual Sunday service was held on board ship, conducted by the captain. During that service, prayers were for those souls who had perished on the *Titanic*, and also for Elizabeth and Edith. On disembarkation from the ship at Liverpool, they caught the train for Southampton, where they stayed for a few days before sailing for Cape Town.

They were sailing from berth forty-eight, which was opposite the now-empty berth forty-three, where the *Titanic* had sailed from just a few months earlier. During their stay in Southampton, Elizabeth wrote to Josephine and Edward in Seattle, thanking them for looking after them when they were there and promising to keep in touch. She also wrote a letter to Edith's eldest stepsister, a Mrs Bosman in Cape Town, informing them of their arrival back in that country.

After boarding the *Carisbrooke Castle* in Southampton Docks, they looked across the dock for a short while at berth forty-three, Elizabeth and Edith finding it hard to believe that just a few months ago, they had been full of excitement as they sailed from there on the *Titanic*. Now they were back here where it had all started. Thomas was gone, and 1,500 other souls had perished along with that beautiful ship, all gone. Edith wanted to blank it out of her mind, but she knew that her mother was still grieving for her father. It was all going to take time. They had a three-week voyage ahead of them. Once back in South Africa, they would pick up the pieces and start all over again.

At daybreak, the *Carisbrooke Castle* slowly passed the breakwater and, on entering the Cape Town docks, made her way into her berth. Edith remembers her mother commenting on seeing Table Mountain again. She said she never thought that they would be back so soon. They were home again, and that was all that mattered. Once on the dockside, they met Edith's stepsister and her husband and were soon on their way to their home. They went up Adderly Street and passed the Mountain View Hotel. It had been, once their hotel and their home before going on that fateful voyage across the Atlantic. On arrival at the Bosman's home, Edith's two step-brothers and her other step-sister met them.

The following days were spent organising Thomas's estate. Edith's stepbrother insisted that Thomas's gold pocket watch was promised to him. Edith remembers her mother's anger at his lack of concern at what they had been through. She told him that he should search the bottom of the North Atlantic if he wanted it so badly.

Some weeks later, the legalities of Thomas's estate had been settled. Solicitors had reached an agreement that all six parties would receive an equal share. The actual figure was never known, but it turned out to be a sizeable sum of money. It became clear that T.W.S. Brown had been quite a wealthy man by all accounts. Once the settlement had been reached, Elizabeth thought it was time to move on. Edith, like her mother, had never really known her father's children from his first marriage, and she was glad to get away.

CHAPTER ELEVEN

RETURN TO SOUTHAMPTON

Fredrick T. Haisman was born at Gloucester Gate, London. As a teenager, he had moved out to Johannesburg with his parents. He spent his earliest days in Itchen, Southampton, England, among the yachts and yachtsmen, the most famous in the world in those days. As a young man he always wanted to go away to sea, but the Victorian values held by his parents insisted that he dismiss such ideas and take up a position as an apprentice draughtsman. His ambition thereafter was to work in the drawing offices of a shipyard or another company involved with the docks and the ship-building industry. This was a difficult profession for him to undertake in a country that had little to offer in the ship-building industry. Perhaps by remaining in England he would have had a far greater future to look forward to in that line of business; however, the decision was not his. He persevered with his studies as an apprenticed junior engineering draughtsman and well suited for the profession at the V.F. & T.P. Company in Johannesburg where he worked.

Fredrick followed with interest the building of the great White Star liners and was horrified at the sinking of the *Titanic*. The press in South Africa at that time was full of the disaster, as was press coverage worldwide, and Fredrick studied every detail that went into print. At this time, a leading newspaper, the *Transvaal Chronicle Limited*, offered a competition to its readership for their ideas for safety at sea, with the *Titanic* disaster in mind. Fredrick entered the competition, enclosing blueprint drawings and sketches of his idea of lifeboats being launched from within the ship's hull, halfway down the ship's side. On 13 May 1912, Fredrick's seventeenth birthday, he received a congratulatory letter from the newspaper, stating that he had won first prize in the competition and inviting him to pick up his winning cheque at their offices. As a result of his efforts, he received favourable comment from the British Board of Trade and the International Life Saving Commission.

The blueprint of his idea showed shell doors opening lower down on the ship's side. Lifeboats were stowed inside the ship's hull on kinds of ramps for easy launching. I can certainly see where he was coming from; he was only a young man at the time, and one must give him credit for his idea. Huge cruise liners today, with their many decks high up on the superstructure, do indeed stow their lifeboats at a much lower level, as it is considered to be far safer and quicker for getting boats away. The ocean liners of yesteryear, with their lifeboat launchings high on the upper decks or boat decks, were time-consuming and cumbersome, and lives had been lost as a consequence. The drawback with Fredrick's design, I have always felt, would have been the loss of much accommodation within the ship's hull. For that reason, it would be out of the question for ship owners and designers to ever consider such an idea.

On the 30 July 1912, the British enquiry into the sinking of the *Titanic* published its findings. Generally, negligence was cited as the main cause of the disaster. The *Titanic's* navigators were considered negligent for allowing the ship to proceed at a speed that was reckless after so many ice warnings had been received. Captain Lord of the *Californian* was negligent for failing to make any rescue attempt after sighting distress rockets, an argument that goes on to this very day. The company was negligent for employing seamen who were inexperienced in the manning of lifeboats, and also negligent for allowing the vessel to sail without sufficient lifeboats on board. The enquiry went on to say that The British Board of Trade was negligent to pass such a vessel to go to sea and negligent in its failure to update the correct requirements for ships of such great tonnage.

The British enquiry, which had opened on 2 May and was conducted by Lord Mersey, had, by the time of its conclusion on

21 June, interviewed over ninety-five witnesses. The majority of those interviewed were crew, with the exception of Sir Cosmo Duff Gordon, who was travelling first class with his wife and secretary. He was questioned closely as to why he had offered money to the crew members in his lifeboat. He replied that the moment the ship had sunk, the crew would have been 'off wages,' and the vessel would have sunk with all their kit on board. He said that he and his wife felt sorry for them and offered a promissory note of five pounds each for them to replace their belongings. It was also noted by the enquiry that their lifeboat only had twelve persons on board, and that they never made any attempt to pick up other survivors.

Perhaps one of the most important witnesses of the proceedings was Second Officer Lightoller, who was asked no less than 1,500 questions throughout the whole enquiry. Being questioned by Mr Scanlon, it was put to him that more crew should have been used in each lifeboat. Lightoller replied that if that had been the case, fewer passengers would have found space in the boats. Mr Scanlon then said that the ship should have carried more lifeboats. Lightoller, questioned about speed, answered that he reckoned the ship was making around 22 knots. He went on to say it was not White Star policy to push their ships hard in their first year of service.

The questioning continued. Mr Scanlon accused the ship's navigating officers of utter recklessness in view of the ice reports received and of the continuing speed of the vessel. Lightoller replied that if that was the case, then all the ships on the North Atlantic trade could also be called reckless. There was the inference from Mr Scanlon that Captain Smith was far too busy socialising instead of being in his rightful place, which was on the bridge. Lightoller answered this by saying there was no truth in such an accusation. He maintained that the captain was always on the bridge for any important decisions or whenever adverse weather conditions prevailed.

Stewardesses were also questioned at the hearing, and they related how they had helped women and children into the boats. One of the stewardesses had previously been on a ship called the *Lake Champlain*, which had also collided with an iceberg, and she knew the emergency procedure for abandoning ship in such an event.

The White Star Line's Mr Bruce Ismay was cleared of all charges made against him, as was Sir Cosmo Duff Gordon for not attempting to rescue anyone. The crew received little mention other than criticism, although three quarters of them had lost their lives. Those who had survived learned that the company had stopped their wages just after midnight, when it was known that the ship was doomed and the company would no longer require their services. It was a disgraceful way to treat the crew. Also disgraceful was the way they were depicted and criticised by numerous books and films over the years, mostly by those who had never been to sea. It was also considered reasonable for the third class to be kept away from boats until the other classes had been accommodated. Such was the class system at the turn of the last century. Not so surprisingly, those classes expected and accepted that kind of treatment.

And so 1912 drew to a close. It was a year that would never be forgotten by many, especially the 705 survivors from the *Titanic* disaster. It had changed their lives, and the lives of those close to them, forever. After years of planning, the great engineering and ship-building achievement that was the *Titanic* had disappeared below the Atlantic in just two hours. There were many lessons to be learned and, as a result, shipping worldwide became far safer. After the enquiry, the *Titanic's* sister ship, the *Olympic,* was immediately fitted with extra lifeboats, as the Board of Trade changed its lifeboat requirement for this new breed of ocean going liner. Mother Nature had dealt a lethal blow to man's complacency with the elements. There had been no wind, no heavy sea, no storm or fog; just one massive iceberg, silently drifting south with the currents to take the lives of over 1,500 souls. It would continue to drift south, slowly getting smaller each day until it eventually became part of the sea, all evidence of the huge mass of floating ice gone forever.

Within months of settling into their new accommodation in Cape Town, Elizabeth began to show signs of becoming generally run down. She displayed a lack of interest in most things. By January 1913 she decided to seek medical advice, realising that her lethargy was affecting her daughter, which was unfair to her. After tests and some lengthy discussions with her doctor, his diagnosis pinpointed the events of the past year as being the main contributory factor for her condition. His recommendation was to have a proper holiday and perhaps go on a cruise.

Elizabeth was dumfounded at his suggestion of going on another sea voyage, but he cited the analogy of the horse and rider; when you fall off, you get right back on again. In contrast to her mother, Edith had been coping quite well over the past year and was now a source of strength for her mother. Elizabeth was beginning to show quite a bit of reliance on her daughter, who was now approaching 17 years of age and becoming a young woman. When Elizabeth told her about the doctor's recommendation of going on a cruise, Edith was equally surprised, especially with her mother's nervous disposition. She was even more surprised when her mother told her several days later that she had taken the doctor's advice and booked a cruise for both of them. It was finally arranged that they set sail on Orient Line's *Orsova,* on a four-week round-trip cruise to Australia.

Edith mentioned little about that actual cruise, other than to say that her mother appeared surprisingly relaxed. The highlight of that cruise was their visit to a medium in Melbourne who had apparently contacted Thomas. The medium, a woman, told them that he was now at peace, along with Rev. Carter. Edith spoke about this meeting throughout her life. She was so convinced by this medium that she always kept a piece of paper with her father's signature on it. When writing her father's signature, the medium wrote in copperplate handwriting which, according to both women, was unmistakeably Thomas's.

So convinced were Elizabeth and Edith that contact had been established with Thomas, they began to feel that they had been meant to go on this cruise in order to meet up with this medium. When their ship left Melbourne that same evening, both women apparently felt a great inner happiness that they had never experienced before. Edith always said that whilst asleep that night, she felt her father's kiss her on her cheek. In the morning, Elizabeth also said that she had felt Thomas's presence, and that he had kissed her gently on the lips at some time during the night.

It goes without saying that in those days, more people were influenced by religion, superstition, and the occult in general. In later years, Edith's family members were mostly cynical about such things, but they always listened to and respected her views.

After the cruise, Elizabeth and her daughter began to settle down again, although it has always been unclear as to when they finally decided to return to Johannesburg. Elizabeth certainly wanted to do something with her life. She had been trained as a young woman in millinery and feather-curling and said she would like to get back into it. They moved to Johannesburg, probably in 1914, and Elizabeth set about going into business on her own. Ostrich feathers were very fashionable at that time, being used for women's hats and costumes, and she could see a good market for her skills. It was at this time that a young gentleman came into her life. He offered his 'expertise' on financial matters and in setting up her own business.

After Elizabeth had put a great deal of money and effort into the business, it just wasn't making a profit. Several months later, she had to abandon the idea and cut her losses. She heard from others that she had been badly advised and had taken on too much too quickly. Her young advisor disagreed. He said that ostrich feathers were not as popular as they once were and if they had continued with the business, it would have been doomed. After the failure of her business venture, Elizabeth continued to see her young 'adviser,' much to Edith's annoyance. He would call on her quite regularly and take her out to dinner or out for the day, leaving Elizabeth to foot the bill most of the time. Edith tried to like her mother's new companion, if only for her mother's sake, but she just felt he was wrong for her. Her father had been twenty years her mother's senior, and this man was twenty years her mother's junior. The most worrying aspect of all was that her money seemed to be the main attraction.

Elizabeth still had a considerable amount of money and was showing a real zest for life. She enjoyed his company and was always prepared to follow whatever plans he had. Edith was happy to see her mother enjoying life once more, but she still felt this man was wrong for her. She knew that it would be a delicate subject to raise with her mother, but she thought it her duty to get through to her before he took every penny. They apparently had some long and difficult discussions about this man in Elizabeth's life, and it was becoming clear that Elizabeth was besotted with him. Edith never knew just how involved her mother was, but she pointedly asked her mother where she thought he would be once her money ran out.

It surprised Elizabeth to find that her daughter was speaking to her about her financial situation and relationship so freely. At the same time, she fully realised that she was doing it because she cared about her welfare. She also realised that Edith was fast approaching womanhood, and was beginning to take after her with her outspoken views and opinions.

From that point onwards, Edith no longer discussed her mother's relationship with her companion and did her best to avoid him. Her mother was obviously obsessed with the man. She knew it didn't matter what she thought of him; nothing was going to change. Shortly after their down-to-earth talk, Elizabeth dropped the bombshell that she was going to marry him. After the shock of hearing that, Edith made up her mind that she would try to show how happy she was for them and expressed her enthusiasm for the impending wedding. They married shortly after Edith's eighteenth birthday, and her mother appeared to be so happy that Edith began to feel guilty at doubting her mother's judgement.

Several months later, things began to change. Her new stepfather began to interfere more into her own private affairs. Edith, always to the point, would remind him that he was married to her mother and not herself. Her dislike for him began to grow over the months.

The following account was always good for a laugh when Edith described it years later, but it does show that she took no nonsense from anyone. Things came to a head one afternoon when Edith had arrived home after buying some new clothes. As she unpacked her bags, he claimed she was spending her money far too freely. He said, 'You don't seem to understand the value of it!'

Edith, feeling that whatever she did with her own money had nothing to do with him, swung round on him and retorted, 'It's none of your business what I do with my money!'

In an attempt to sound fatherly, he replied, 'If you were my daughter, I would put you on a fixed allowance until you knew better.'

'You're not my father, thank God!' Edith shot back. Raising her voice, she went on. 'The only reason you are here is to satisfy your own drinking habits!' She pointed her finger at him and shouted, 'Don't you ever forget that it's my father's money that you are living off of in the first place!'

With that, her new stepfather bowed mockingly toward her and sneeringly replied, 'Then I take my hat off to your dear departed father.' Straightening up, he followed that by sticking up two fingers in a rude gesture.

Edith exploded, lunging forward; she slapped him across the face as hard as she could. This fury from such a small woman took him utterly by surprise, knocking him off balance and causing him to almost fall over a chair close by. Quickly, putting his hand up to his stinging face, he spun on his heel and stormed out of the room.

This was the beginning of a period when Edith realised that she could no longer live under the same roof as her stepfather. If she stayed there, it would continue to cause arguments. She apologised to her mother for her outburst. She said that when he insulted her father, she just lost control. Elizabeth hated having any kind of argument with her daughter and tried her best to keep the peace between the two of them. She also knew that Edith was now a grown woman; perhaps the time had come for her to start making a life for herself. She also knew that Edith and her stepfather would never get on together.

Edith had told her mother in no uncertain terms that this man's drinking habits would drag them all down until they had nothing left. It was arranged that Edith would move out and live with some friends of theirs in Johannesburg of whom they knew from Cape Town many years ago. Edith and her mother parted on good terms and remained as close as ever, despite living apart for the first time in their lives. They would arrange meetings together, or Edith would visit her mother when she knew her stepfather wasn't there, and it seemed to work perfectly well. Edith began to get out and about more with her friend Kathryn. She was the daughter of their friends of who she was now living and was of the same age. They found the Wemmer Pan Sailing club's monthly functions a good venue to enjoy a night out once in a while.

With his interest in the sea, Fredrick Haisman, took up sailing, joining his father, Fred Haisman, in the Wemmer Pan Sailing Club and taking part in many regattas. In 1914, skippering the *Ruby*, he won the Dr Frood Commodore Cup with Mr Harry Tugwell, who was at that club for the season. It was during this period that our father met Robert Hichens, the quartermaster who had been at the wheel of the *Titanic* at the time of the collision with the iceberg. They remained friends for some time due to our father's interest in the *Titanic*, and, no doubt, their interests in regattas and small boats generally.

In April 1917 the fifth anniversary of the sinking of the *Titanic* was approaching, and each month the Wemmer Pan Sailing Club held a social evening for friends and families of members. It was at this function that Edith Brown met Fredrick Haisman. After a courtship of just six weeks, they married in Johannesburg on 30 June 1917. Over the following weeks, Mrs Edith Eileen Haisman, as she was now called, would learn a great deal about Fredrick Thankful Haisman and his family background.

Fred Haisman, sen. was a cycle engineer and a close associate of Dan Rudge and Thomas Humber, well-known cycle manufacturers in England at that time. It was claimed that Fred Haisman was one of the pioneers of the Velocipede Boneshaker bicycle. When he died in 1939, there was coverage in the *Cape Times,on December 20, 1939*, and also in the *Southampton Echo on February 3, 1940*. The coverage in the Southampton newspaper was much the same as shown here, but it added that when in Southampton, his workshop was situated at the Back- Of –The- Walls. It went on to mention his winning a gold medal in cycling at the B-P-C-C in 1892. He later came associated with Byrne, and founded Byrne-Haisman Cycles under Royal Letters Patent. There was also mention of his opening the Camps Bay Pavillion in the Cape Province, which staged one of the first professional boxing matches held in South Africa, a bout between Pedlar Palmer and W. Austin.

DEATH OF MR. FRED HAISMAN

Pioneer in making cycles

Mr. Fred Haisman who claimed to be one of the pioneers of the velocipede and 'boneshaker' has just died in Johannesburg aged 80. He was well known to many old residents and a great fund of anecdote. He had been working since the age of eleven. Mr. Haisman used to speak proudly of his early association with the velocipede.

Born in London he was a blacksmith by trade. During the 1870 Franco-German War he assisted a blacksmith in Southampton to make velocipedes, and later was instrumental in bringing about the manufacture of the 'bone-shaker.' His next effort was the medium-height ordinary bicycle, which gradually led up to the safety bicycle.

Mr. Haisman claimed to have made the first safety bicycle for military purposes. That was in 1887. He submitted his machine to a test by officials of the British War Office, and as a result an order was placed for a large number of safety bicycles. He exhibited machines at the Crystal Palace in 1886 and at the Paris exhibition in 1889. It was after the war office passed his machine in 1887 that he put the first modern cycle frame on the market for sale to the general public.

When the South African war broke out he helped to raise funds in London for the beleaguered garrison in Mafeking and was publicly thanked by the then Prince of Wales, later King Edward V11.

Mr Haisman came to South Africa in 1900, on the maiden voyage of the Saxon, the famous Union Castle mail boat. The war was still on and Mr. Haisman's knowledge of cycles was of considerable value to the British Military Command. He was given charge of the Cape Colony Cycle Corps and remained in the service for the brief period of 81 days when the war ended.

Mr. Haisman came to the Rand in 1903, went back to Cape Town for a short period during which time he opened the Camps Bay Pavilion, and then returned to Johannesburg in 1904. A year later he opened the Constitutional Club in Jeppe. The membership rose to 2,000 and included the late Sir George Farrar and other well-known men at that time.

Mr. Haisman has remained on the Rand since. He was ever a fine craftsman in iron. He had his own autobiography almost completed at the time of his death.

The funeral will take place today.

Shortly after getting married, Fredrick and Edith bought a place in Johannesburg, and life for both of them was blissfully happy. They had a wide circle of friends and a good social life. They spent many hours sailing, and at the end of the day enjoyed cocktails and meals at the sailing club. At this time, Fredrick began building his own sailing boat, and it was considered by many in the sailing community to be a fine boat when finished. Edith saw less of her mother after her marriage, but she appeared happy enough each time she visited her. On one of her visits, her stepfather was there, and she noticed that her mother had been drinking. This was unlike her, as she had hardly touched alcohol when married to Thomas. Perhaps a dry sherry after dinner, or something similar, was all she would ever drink. If her mother was happy, then Edith had no intention of interfering in her life, although on leaving, she gave her stepfather a look that left him in no doubt at what she thought.After the birth of Fredrick, Jr. in Johannesburg in 1918, Fredrick and Edith began to discuss their future, particularly Fredrick's work prospects. It had always been well known that Edith was the driving force behind Fredrick. She insisted that he attend night school to further his career prospects. Although they were well settled and loved South Africa, in those days there just wasn't much work there in shipbuilding and dock construction. During this period, shipbuilding in Britain appeared undeterred by the loss of the *Titanic.* Another huge liner called the *Aquitania* had been built, and she would also be used on the North Atlantic service.

By 1920, Fredrick and Edith decided to sell up in Johannesburg and travel to England. They settled in Southampton in order for Fredrick to pursue his career in the docks, engineering, and shipbuilding business. He worked under the chief engineer, Wentworth-Shields. There was to be a huge docks-rebuilding program in Southampton called the New Docks Scheme, which would be of several years' duration. This was to be Southampton's answer to the great new passenger liners that were destined for the port.

On their last day in Johannesburg, they went to see Elizabeth. After what they had been through together it was a sad occasion for both women. Unknown to them both, this would be the last time they would ever see each other.

Fredrick and Edith sailed from Cape Town on the *Saxon,* a Union Castle Line ship that Edith had sailed on before and a ship she liked. After leaving Cape Town, she discovered that she was pregnant with her second child.

After three weeks at sea, they arrived in Southampton. This must have been quite an emotional experience, especially for Edith. The *Saxon* had arrived at berth forty-eight, just a few berths from where, eight years previously, she had set sail on the *Titanic* with her mother and father on a voyage that was to offer them all a new life in America.

Whenever she was asked about her feelings at that time, Edith always talked about the wives and children in Southampton who must have suffered the loss of their loved ones.

Once settled back in England, Edith's second son, Kenneth, was born in February 1921. Life in England turned out to be much harder than she had anticipated. Fredrick was working and attending night school as well. Gone were the days where servants were the norm for all whites and Edith spent her time helping her mother and father around their hotel. In those days, she never considered going out to work for a living or doing mundane jobs like housework. It was never deemed necessary; the future held better things for her.

However, this was not the case in England, as Edith soon found out. She had to teach herself how to cook and perform other household chores totally unfamiliar to her. She never complained as she went about making bread, ironing, starching and turning Fredrick's collars, scrubbing floors, and cleaning. She learned to black lead the stove, save some coals after cleaning the grate, and keep the draughts around the doors and windows at bay. She never complained. She had a determination to succeed in everything she did, and she always kept a clean and tidy home.

In February 1923 a third son was born to Edith. He was named Geoffrey, and it was a busy time for her. Generally, life was good. Fredrick was in work, which was something to be envied in those days. There were well over a million unemployed in the early 1920s and '30s, and 350,000 of them were servicemen who had been lucky enough to have arrived back home alive at the end of it all. Mass unemployment was their reward for service to their country.

Throughout the past four years, Edith had kept in regular touch with her mother back in Johannesburg, although her letters were becoming less frequent as time went on. The letters she did receive from her mother showed she was reasonably happy, although her writing was becoming untidy. In January 1925 a fourth son was born to Fredrick and Edith, and they named him Leo. After his birth, they decided to move to a larger house in Leighton Road, Sholing, a suburb of Southampton. Letters from Elizabeth in Johannesburg were becoming fewer by the end of 1925, which caused Edith some concern. Her handwriting was becoming worse, although her letters gave no indication that anything was wrong. Edith had never liked or trusted her stepfather and, at times, wondered just what kind of life he was giving her mother. She knew that they owned a bottle store somewhere in Johannesburg and it was clear that her stepfather would have been behind such a business. It would have been paid for, with what would have been, the last of her mother's money.

During the first week of July 1926, Edith received a letter from her stepsister saying that her mother had passed away in hospital in Salisbury, Rhodesia, 29 June 1926, aged just 53. Edith felt that her mother and father were together again. She always felt that her mother had never fully gotten over losing her beloved Thomas on the *Titanic*.

Edith's two daughters, Dorothy and Joy, were named appropriately when Joy, the eldest, finally arrived several years after the births of their four sons, Fredrick, Kenneth, Geoffrey, and Leo.

Edith had been desperately hoping for a girl and decided that the arrival of her first daughter was a joyous occasion. Dorothy, the seventh child born, was named after Edith's sister, who had sadly died from diphtheria at just 8 years of age back in Cape Town in 1908. The other two sons, John and Donald, were numbers six and eight in the line up, respectively. Brian, the second-youngest son, was number nine, and David, the author, came along as the last born at number ten.

As 1930 approached, there was little said about the *Titanic* disaster. It had taken its place in the history books as one of the worst disasters in maritime history. Edith only spoke about it when prompted by someone or when her children asked. Other than that, for the time being, it had been laid to rest.

During the early part of the 1930s, the Cunard Line began to move their ships down to Southampton from Liverpool. As a result, many crewmembers made their homes in the port. One of those was Captain Rostron of the *Carpathia*, who went on to command other ships of the line until his retirement. He was rightfully looked upon as a hero in his day, due to his immediate response and navigation through treacherous ice conditions to save *Titanic's* passengers.

When the children were young, most of the discipline was carried out by Edith, who wouldn't hesitate to wallop them with whatever came to hand if she thought they deserved it. She was also strict at the table and made sure the children observed the good manners she had laid down for them. This was clearly a reflection on her own upbringing. Failure to observe the rules would result in the offender receiving a rap across the knuckles with the ever-present wooden spoon kept at her side for that purpose.

With half a dozen hungry kids at table during meal times, actions spoke louder than words, and it never appeared to do them any harm. Looking back, it was clear that Fredrick and Edith had done their level best in raising their ten children. Apart from getting into all kinds of mischief now and then, none of them ever got into any serious trouble.

In 1932, the Depression was having a great effect on people's lives. Many were out of work and struggling to feed their families. The eldest son, Fredrick, Jr., had joined the Royal Navy and was sent to St Vincent's Training College at Portsmouth, as did Kenneth and Geoffrey. It was an interesting time for Geoffrey. As a boy seaman, he received six of the best across his backside for being late for duty, and the discipline meted out in those days was seldom forgotten. He mentioned years later that he was never late again, whatever the circumstances.

In 1933, work was started on the world's largest liner ever, the 81,000-ton *R.M.S. Queen Mary*, a ship almost twice the size of the *Titanic*. She would, in years to come, be one of the world's favourite passenger liners across the Atlantic. It was during this time that the *Georgic* and *Brittanic* were the last ships to be built for White Star Line; by 1934 the company had amalgamated with the Cunard Steamship Company, later to be known as the Cunard White Star Company.

On 3 September 1939, Britain and France declared war on Germany. Within hours of that declaration, air raid sirens could be heard in England for the first time. This was causing concern to all families with sons and daughters of an age for military service.

The Haisman family had their four eldest sons serving in the war. That in itself was a worry for them, but other families were in the same situation. There was the added concern of not only losing a loved one when away at war but of being bombed out of your home as well. Southampton was a strategic target for the Luftwaffe, with its docks and Supermarine seaplane base, which had become subjected to heavy bombing raids. Fredrick was an air-raid warden; he would be out most nights, ensuring blackout regulations were being adhered to, whilst Edith remained at home with the younger ones. In January 1942 rationing, mainly of dairy products and sugar, but later on, many more food items were added to the list. Throughout this period, the Luftwaffe blitzed Britain with extensive bombing in Coventry, London, and Southampton, along with other important cities.

In 1942, David, the youngest child, was admitted to hospital for a hernia operation. The Luftwaffe was bombing Southampton heavily, and hospitals were being targeted. When air raids were imminent, it was thought it would be far safer to move patients home if they could be moved, rather than leave them in hospital. David's brother Leo came to collect him and literally carried him home during an air raid, going right across Southampton from the South Hants Hospital to their home in Sholing, a distance of around three miles.

Brian, who was two years older than David, was also in hospital in Southampton when it was bombed during the war. He suffered from shell shock and never fully recovered mentally. His speech was unintelligible at times, causing him to throw many tantrums out of frustration. He became grossly overweight as he got older. It was the opinion of several doctors that he would eventually have to go into care. Edith would have none of it. She always maintained that she knew how to look after him better than anyone else, insisting that he would always remain at home with the rest the family. Despite his handicap, he was a good-looking, fair-skinned boy, loved by everyone and, most of the time, lots of fun to the younger ones.

He was, however, hard work for Edith, who never complained. She continued to take care of him until he died suddenly from heart failure at just 14 years of age. Although the elder sons were serving in the armed forces during the war and there was much bombing in Southampton, it turned out that Brian was the only war casualty the family suffered. But it must have been a trying time for the Haisman family.

Edith, according to the elder members of her family and those who knew her, showed little fear of the Southampton air raids. At the time, many people were erecting Anderson shelters in their gardens. These were tunnel-shaped structures of corrugated iron. As they were dug in below ground level, they were considered safer during the bombing raids than remaining in the home.

Fredrick had shored up the ceilings and other parts of the house with timber in an effort to compensate for any weaknesses in the building that might develop from the constant bombing raids in the area. Edith, however, would never go into the shelter in the back garden during air raids. She considered the underground structures death traps. 'We could all end up being buried alive,' she said. It took tremendous persuasion by her husband to get her to go in there when the bombing became really intensive. At that time, everyone had been instructed to carry gas masks wherever they went. The younger ones had gas masks modelled on a Mickey Mouse look-alike, but despite that, they still hated wearing them.

On some mornings after those raids, the children still going to school would arrive there to find troops, or families that had been bombed out of their homes during the night, asleep in the classrooms. Southampton was one of the most heavily bombed cities along the south coast, being targeted because of its docks, shipping supply routes, and Supermarine flying boat station. During those bombing campaigns, some 3,600 buildings were destroyed. A further 40,000 were damaged, and 650 people were killed. This was the result of 2,630 high-explosive bombs and around 31,000 incendiary devices. Throughout that period, over 2 million US troops and 1.5 million Allied forces used the port.

During air raids, Fredrick and Edith had a set plan to get all of the children under the stairs or under the tables. This was a well-tried practice by many householders. Even if the bomb hit several streets away, falling plaster or masonry could cause injuries, and being under the stairs or tables would provide some shelter from falling debris. When Fredrick was out patrolling the streets to ensure the blackout was being observed, Edith would ensure that all the children were safely tucked up into their little havens before she went up to bed alone. She always maintained that Hitler would never keep her out of her bed at night, whatever the outcome.

Sometimes during air raids, neighbours would make their way to their house, as they seemed to derive some sort of security within their home. At those times, Edith was always pressed to tell them stories of when she was a young girl in South Africa, her convent education, and the circle of wealthy friends her father had around him. They could never get enough of listening of her *Titanic* experiences. They found a kind of comfort from those stories, which probably took their minds off of the bombings and their menfolk away fighting the war.

Late one night during an air raid, there was a direct hit on the railway line at the bottom of the hill, and the blast blew out many windows in the neighbourhood. There was broken glass everywhere, but as luck would have it, none of the children were injured. Edith quickly came downstairs and calmed everyone down. When the all clear was sounded, she arranged for everyone to sleep upstairs for the rest of the night and set about the task of clearing up the mess scattered throughout the house.

Most of the air raids were at night, but as the war progressed, the Germans decided that daytime raids were also necessary. It was becoming clear that Britain was a tougher nut to crack than first thought. On one such raid, Edith was out in the garden hanging up washing when she suddenly looked up and noticed the sky was full of enemy aircraft dropping bombs over the whole area. The air raid sirens had been late in giving out warnings, so she shouted to all the kids to make a dash indoors for cover and to dive under the tables and the cupboard under the stairs. During this particular raid, Southampton Docks was badly hit. Many were killed, and the fires burned for a week. It was announced that it was likely that this intensive bombing would continue unabated over the docks in the days and weeks to come. This warning was aimed specifically at those living in the neighbourhoods around the Supermarine base at Woolston and others living within close proximity of dockland in general. These families were warned to get completely away from Southampton.

The Haisman home was not far from Woolston, so it was decided that they should get away from the place as soon as possible. That night, Fredrick, Edith, and six children, and Nip, the family dog, walked far out into the countryside to put as much distance as possible between themselves and the docks. In the early hours of the morning, they ended up outside of a great old country pub. The landlady invited them in and allowed them to sleep on the pub floor until daybreak. In the morning she brought them bacon and eggs, which was appreciated by all after trudging across the countryside throughout the best part of the night.

After this latest assault on Southampton, it was decided by the authorities that all children should be evacuated to outlying country districts for their safety. This could have meant many parents being separated from their children for lengthy periods, something Edith, more so than Fredrick, just wasn't happy about. But she knew it was in their best interests. It was decided that the older ones would go and the youngest, Brian and David, would remain with them. The day came for the evacuees to be taken to Southampton's Central Station to catch a train to the West Country, and it was an upsetting time for all. On arrival at the station, they were all given identification labels to pin on their coats. After many tearful goodbyes, the train pulled away as children wept and waved from the carriage windows. It goes without saying just how homesick they all were, but within a few months they were returned home.

During this whole period of uncertainty, Fredrick was working for the Admiralty in Portsmouth. He and Edith decided they should move to a village called West Wittering, not far from Chichester but deemed as somewhat safer than Southampton. It was learned some years later that their house in Southampton was sold for a give-away price; quite naturally, people just weren't buying property whilst the war was ongoing. On moving to West Wittering, they did manage to buy a café in the village called 'The Cherries Café.' It was the only café in West Wittering at that time and it was mainly supported by Canadian troops. The only other place where people could get together was in the only pub in the village, called 'The Old House At Home,' which was about as far as the entertainment went.

The whole village was surrounded by farmland, and just down the lane from their Café' was as a beach, which the children visited frequently. In many respects, they were quite fortunate to live in that area and to have their father working at Portsmouth dockyard and home every night.

In 1943, Fredrick received a posting abroad to Simonstown in South Africa. It was arranged by the Admiralty that the family would follow him out at a later date. This was a break for all concerned. Edith was understandably thrilled to know that she would be going back to her beloved South Africa and getting the children away from the war in England. Fredrick sailed from Liverpool on a French ship, which they learned later was a floating disaster with crew trouble and breakdowns. It finally ran aground off of Cape Town six weeks later. Edith was hoping they would all be going to join him within a few months, but it wasn't to be. It turned out to be a wait of over a year, and in that time things didn't go as well as she would have hoped.

Many years later, when the children were old enough to appreciate the circumstances, they realised just how much anguish and worry she must have gone through. As the war raged on, there were long periods without receiving any mail from the four elder sons away at sea. Being separated from her husband for the first time in twenty-six years was of no comfort to her either. During that period, Geoff, the third-eldest son, arrived home on survivor's leave after being bombed and torpedoed at sea. He arrived unannounced one afternoon, wearing his navy bell-bottom trousers and a US army jacket and looking a bit of a mess. He just wanted to sleep for a week. Leo, the fourth-eldest son, was running supplies to Murmansk and Archangel with Russian convoys. Little was heard from him for months, which was also a worry. The eldest son, Fredrick, Jr., was reported missing in action, but a week later had apparently escaped from a prisoner of war camp and was safe.

In late 1944, a letter arrived from the Admiralty confirming that arrangements were under way for the rest of the family to rejoin Fredrick in Simonstown, but the exact details were being kept secret. There was a great deal of excitement at that time as they packed and prepared for their eventual train journey to Swansea. On arrival there, a huge surge of women factory workers swarmed across the station toward the carriage doors of the train as it drew to a halt. A station porter, who had spotted them, pushed through the crowds to help Edith with the children as they crossed the platform to relative safety in the waiting room. A policeman was on hand to escort them away from the station and to help them in finding 'digs' for the night prior to their boarding the troop ship they would be sailing on. Everyone was feeling utterly miserable. They were cold and tired from walking the streets of Swansea in search of accommodation. They eventually found somewhere to spend the night. All six of them and Edith crowded into one room, where they were to spend a cold sleepless night before an early morning call for their ship.

Their ship, the *Empire Grace*, as it was learned later, was a vessel of some 13,000 tons, built by Harland and Wolff of Belfast for the Australian and New Zealand service but commissioned by the British government for troop transport. On leaving Swansea, they sailed up to Greenock to take on board five hundred troops bound for St Helena in the South Atlantic. Once again, Edith found herself back at sea, this time with six of her own children to keep her company and a dangerous voyage ahead.

With such a large number of troops on board, the ship was a valuable target and, as the North Atlantic was well known for German U-boat activity, it was essential that they have a convoy escort them some of the way. Heading into the Bay of Biscay, the younger children were quite surprised by all the grey ships around them when they came up on deck early each morning. It was at that time that the sea began to take on a fascination that remained with some of them for the rest of their lives. They would stare out to sea as each vessel in turn would pitch into the heavy seas, throwing spray and surplus water all over their forward decks. Rising up, the seawater and spray would begin to clear away from their forward decks before the vessels plunged into the sea again. Edith had her work cut out keeping an eye on the younger ones. Getting too close to the ship's rail was definitely out of bounds as far as she was concerned.

Early in the voyage, the troops had rigged up a swing for the kids from an awning spar on the after deck, and this became one of their favourite places onboard ship. For the youngsters, there was little else to do on a ship like that, and with the troops always having a bit of a laugh with them, they looked forward to it each day. Besides, looking back, one can imagine that the soldiers onboard, heading for an uncertain future, used that time to take their minds off of the tasks that might lie ahead for them in St Helena. Coming up on deck as usual early one morning off of the south-western tip of Portugal, the children were amazed to find an empty sea around them. There was not a single ship in sight. They were to learn later that during the night, the convoy had altered course and headed for the Straits of Gibraltar, leaving the *Empire Grace* to continue on its southerly course, completely blacked out at night and now on her own.

Just a few days after the convoy left them, they were put on 'action stations' several times over the following days, as it was feared a German U-boat was shadowing the ship. They were all instructed to turn in at night fully dressed. Sometimes, after being roused from their sleep, they were made to sit outside in the passageway with a life jacket on until told it was all right to go back to bed. On one occasion, they had to go up on the boat deck with blankets and wait until the all-clear was given before being able to return to their cabin. On those occasions, Edith did her best to keep the younger children occupied. Years later, they would realize how she must have felt, possibly facing another shipwreck, this time with six of her children. But the elder members of the family always said that she appeared to carry on as normal despite what dangers lay ahead.

Several days later, as they sailed further into the South Atlantic, the U-boat threat subsided, but complete blackout routine at night was continued throughout the remainder of the voyage.

Three and half weeks after leaving Greenock, the *Empire Grace* dropped anchor off of St Helena, a small volcanic island approximately 1,700 miles northwest of Cape Town. This was the island to which Napoleon had been sent in exile. In 1944, this island had a population of around 4,500, and now they had another 500 British troops for their protection. During their brief stay at St Helena, the younger children experienced fruit they had never set eyes on before. They always remembered the youngest son eating his first banana. He tackled this fruit with the skin on before his eldest sister snatched it out of his hand and told him that he should peel the thing first!

After the troops had gone ashore in barges, there was a kind of emptiness and sadness, as many friendships had been made during the voyage.

They arrived in Cape Town a few days later and were soon reunited with Fredrick, who met them on the dockside. For Edith, it must have been a great relief to be reunited with her husband and to know that her children were destined for a better future. Before disembarking, Edith had a conversation with a ship's officer, commenting on the periods of 'action stations' during the voyage. It was learned later that during this short exchange with the officer, she mentioned her *Titanic* experience and said she couldn't imagine a repeat performance, this time with six of her children. His casual reply was that there was little to worry about, as a soldier had been designated to her and each child if they had to abandon ship. Apparently, she replied that she would have appreciated it more had she been told about it at the time! Fredrick, with his dry sense of humour, said to Edith that it was ironic that every time she got on a ship, they had to take to the lifeboats!

There was a lot of excitement that day, with the strangeness of their new surroundings and the prospect of a whole new world opening up before them. The train ride from Cape Town to Simonstown was an adventure to them all. It was their first time travelling on an electric train, and the beautiful sandy beaches and coastline that swept past their carriage windows. They would laugh each time the train sounded its horn. It reminded them of an air raid siren when a bombing raid was imminent back in Southampton, but that was a thing of the past. Photos of Simonstown today still show it as unspoiled. It remains a pretty little township situated on the side of a mountain overlooking Simons Bay. It was named after Simon van der Stelle, the Dutch governor back in 1679, who also had the township of Stellenbosch, named after him, which is situated just outside of Cape Town.

Their first home in Simonstown was named Newry Villa. It was a bungalow-style home situated on high ground at the top of a hill called Quarry Road, the position offering a fine view of Simons Bay and the naval dockyard. The road got its name from the quarry, which was further up the mountainside some distance behind their house. This was a happy home for all of them, and it was from here that the four youngest children started their education at Simonstown Secondary School. Education was good at the school, although the Afrikaans teachers were very strict, and the Afrikaans language was part of the curriculum. Their attempts to read or write the language were usually followed by a slap about the head, the pulling of hair, or a ruler smacking the backs of their legs until they got it right. Another 'persuader' the male teachers used on the boys was to wrench up on one of their sideburns until they were standing on tiptoe. They would then bellow into the boy's ear until he understood why he was being subjected to this form of so-called discipline.

The teachers frequently spoke Afrikaans between themselves, sometimes using Afrikaans and English in the same sentence. As far as they were concerned, this was no excuse for not understanding them. After a few slaps about the head, an occasional punch, or a bit of hair pulling, it becomes quite amazing just how quickly one can pick up the lingo under those circumstances. One fiery Afrikaans female teacher laid into them more than the rest, and they were all terrified of her. She would call them out to stand alongside of her at her desk and would continually slap the backs of their legs with a ruler. She wouldn't stop until she had received the right answers to her questions. When she had finished and the pupils were sent back to their desks, the backs of their legs would be taking on a mottled, black and blue appearance. They could never forget that woman, having been the recipients of many an encounter with her ruler. Much later, they became convinced that she must have been a test pilot in a broom factory at some time or other!

Away from the trials and tribulations of school life, home life had its moments whilst living in Quarry Road. On occasion, they would be raided by baboons searching for food and scavenging about if they were careless enough to leave the place open when they were out. The baboons would enter the house and ransack just about everything. On returning home, the family knew that they had had visitors by the dung-like smell that had been left behind. This only happened to them in their early days of living in Simonstown, before they really knew what those animals were capable of. They had two dogs in those days, named Nip and Nap, and they had a habit of chasing the baboons whenever they saw them in the back garden. Everyone did their best to prevent this, as baboons could become quite aggressive and could easily kill a dog if they were surprised or cornered.

Those problems weren't to last, however, as they moved after a year to an Admiralty house called, quite simply, residence no. 28. This house had bars on all the downstairs windows to safeguard against marauding baboons, and it was here that they would remain for the next four years of their stay in South Africa. Their new home was a much bigger place than Newry Villa, situated at the end of a cul-de-sac at the top of a slight hill. This higher elevation was supported by a wall of rocks cemented together with steps to one side, leading up to the front garden. On the right of the steps was a building known as the mortuary. The whole place had once been used by the Royal Navy as a shore-based sickbay. The whole house had walls three feet thick and was constructed with material from the same quarry as Newry Villa. The garden had no boundary fence but gently sloped up, becoming part of the mountainside and offering views of the quarry and beyond.

Life in Simonstown for Europeans (or 'Whites,' as they were generally known) meant that just about all of them had a house servant or home help of local origin. For the Haisman family, it was no different in that respect, as Fredrick received an allowance from the Admiralty for such a person to help in the home. They had employed several home helps before finding someone suitable. His name was Josiah, and he eventually turned out to be really good about the place and was treated almost like one of the family. His accommodation was at the back of the house, in his own detached building. The younger children spent a lot of time in there, talking to him about his 'two wives and children up country,' as he would say.

Old Joe, as they knew him, was of slim build and quite tall. He had a clipped moustache and was of tribal origin. He was a likeable character and got on very well with Fredrick, who always gave him a brandy or two when cooking the Sunday lunch. Sometimes he would have one too many and lurch about the kitchen doing his chores, much to everyone's amusement.

In 1945, the war ended, and there was jubilation just about everywhere. Many parties followed. For the younger ones, life went on much the same. They continued to do their usual things, although they heard many times, that things would be changing for the better. The two younger boys would spend a great deal of time in Simonstown Dockyard, just walking around and looking at the different warships moored up alongside of the quay. There was never any problem with them going in and out of the dockyard in those days; they knew the dock police and were quite friendly with all of them.

Now that the war had ended, the Royal Navy was slowly running down its fleet. Many ships like *HMS Neiride, HMS Actaeon, HMS Norfolk,* and the *HMS Birmingham* were returning to England, leaving the docks looking quite empty. The two younger sons became more focused on fishing, generally messing around the beaches, and mountain climbing with their elder brothers or friends. The two daughters, Joy and Dorothy, were beginning to find some of the younger naval ratings around the town of some interest.

It was around 1946 that the three elder brothers serving in the Royal Navy were all in Simonstown at the same time. Leo, the fourth-eldest in the merchant navy, managed to get a ship out to South Africa with Union Castle Line. For the first time in 12 years, the whole family was together. It would never happen again, which was a great pity, but at the time they had much to talk about.

In 1947, the Royal Family visited South Africa, arriving in Cape Town on *HMS Vanguard,* Britain's largest warship at that time. They were accompanied by the two princesses, Elizabeth and Margaret.

Simonstown was included in their itinerary, and the small township did its best to welcome the royal visitors. Sailors in white uniforms were lined up on either side of the main road right through the whole town. Crowds began to gather on the pavements on both sides. It was a beautiful, sunny day, and all the local dignitaries stood in small groups, nervously shuffling around and waiting for the big moment. After the Royals had met all those who had to be met, they went on to Admiralty House for lunch before leaving.

During the year of 1947, the history books recorded that Europe was gradually recovering from the devastation of World War Two, but Britain was in the grip of one of the worst winters ever recorded. It was a winter the 'old country' could have well done without. There was a further tightening on food rationing, and many items in the shops returned to wartime scarcity. On a lighter note, it was announced that Princess Elizabeth would marry her Greek fiancé, Prince Phillip.

On May 8, 1947, Simonstown's weekly magazine, ran an article on Edith's experiences on the *Titanic*. For the first time, many in the family began to take in the significance of that disaster. It was because of that disaster that the family came into being. Had it not been for the *Titanic*, Edith's life would have been entirely different. For a popular magazine to write an article about her caused all of them to feel quite proud of her, and she became the talk of the town in no time at all. In a small township like Simonstown, this was an interesting article for the local residents, as Edith was the only South African survivor from the *Titanic*.

Up until that time, Edith never really spoke about it unless someone brought the subject up first, so they always thought it was just their own family story and never gave it much thought. Naturally, after the magazine article, the family began to realize how the public viewed the story. They, too, began to ask many more questions and look closer into the story. A full text of that article is shown here, along with some errors in the write-up regarding the depth of water in Lifeboat 14, which wouldn't have been quite possible under the circumstances. The boat did leak throughout the night, though, despite continuous bailing by the boat's crew, and Edith always spoke of how her precious button-up leather boots were ruined. This was to be their first experience as children of how the public viewed their mother's experiences and how the *Titanic* continually came back into her life as the years went by.

Here is a copy of the article as it appeared.

THE OUTSPAN(1947) Pages 7-8

A South African Woman Describes The World's Greatest Shipping Disaster.

The recent shipwrecks off of the South African coast have reminded me that I am, I think, the only South African survivor of the greatest shipping disaster of all time, the sinking of the Titanic.

I was born at the Masonic Hotel, Worcester in 1896, my father, the late TWS Brown then being the proprietor of the hotel. Between that time and that of our departure for the USA, my father took out several hotels at Bloemfontein, Colesburg and the Mountain View Hotel in Cape Town.

Towards the end of 1911 my father decided to join my mother's relatives in Seattle and take up business there, and in consequence he disposed of nearly all his assets here.

We sailed for England early in 1912 and duly arrived in London, where we stayed up to the time of departure. One day our father told us that he had booked our passage on the RMS Titanic which was due to sail from Southampton about April the 11th.

Father had insured our belongings for our passage from the Cape, but although he spent a considerable amount on hotel equipment in London, he did not insure for the trip to the USA.

Upon arrival at the dockside, I, as a child of sixteen, was completely amazed at the vastness of this modern wonder of shipbuilding skill. She was the Queen Mary of her day, and, incidentally, only about 140 feet shorter in length. Her tonnage was about 46,000 as near as I can remember and she had ten decks. One of the public rooms could accommodate about 400 persons. It was no wonder that the public and officials thought her to be unsinkable.

As the Titanic's mooring ropes were being cast off, disaster nearly overtook us with an American ship in an opposite berth. The mooring ropes at one end of the other liner snapped and she swung out towards us. This was no doubt due to the suction of our propellers. I remember my father saying this was a bad start.

The first day out or two we naturally came into contact with some of the other passengers, and I remember being introduced to Mr Murdoch, one of the officers, who was on the bridge at the time of the disaster.

On the night of the 14th we felt that the temperature was dropping very considerably, but little did we realise that this was due to the presence of icebergs. We turned in about 10.30. We couldn't have been asleep very long when the ship giving a shudder awakened me. This would have been about 11.30, and in a very short time we felt that the engines had stopped. My father then came to us and said: 'You had better get up and dressed.'

We went on deck and found the night very still and clear, but there seemed to be no excitement, only some fragments lying about on deck. I began to notice at this early stage that we were slightly down at the head and had a very small list to one side. We noticed what we thought to be ship's lights in the distance.

It was very difficult to make conversation owing to the terrific noise of escaping steam. The boat deck was now becoming busy as the boats were being prepared, and the order for 'women and children first' convinced us that all was not well.

There was little or no panic except for some gesticulating at the steerage end of the ship. Among those I saw that were taking things very calmly were Colonel JJ Astor and his bride, Mr WT Stead and Mr. and Mrs. Strauss. My father came to us and said we had better go to our boat, which I believe was no. 13. He led us to it and kissed us and said, 'I will see you in New York. Don't worry.' We never saw him again.

Whilst precautions were being made to lower our boat, I scrambled out to try and find my father, but was not successful. Upon my return to the boat station I saw that the boat was being lowered and that I was prevented from joining my mother. However, being a small person I managed to elude those trying to stop me and jumped. More by luck than judgement I landed in the boat. By the time we had pulled away from the ship it was evident that she was doomed.

The fore part of the ship was under water nearly as far as the bridge, and the most remarkable thing was the lights were burning under water, and these did not go out until the ship took her final plunge. We could still hear the band playing and they continued to do so until nearly the end. We began to feel very cold as the temperature was well below freezing and to make matters worse, I felt the water gradually creeping up my legs and although the crew kept bailing all through the night, the water never went far below my ankles. As the great ship began to show signs of taking her final plunge, the shrieks and cries were heard and this went on for some considerable time after the ship had disappeared.

The night was so clear that one could see hundreds of people in the water and I should say many were killed by the shock and when the forward funnel fell over this must have accounted for many more. There was a terrific roar as the engines and boilers broke loose owing to the steepness of the ship's position, she was now nearly vertical. At about a quarter to two she finally slid below the surface and left a few boatloads of passengers and hundreds struggling in the water crying for help, which never came as it would have been dangerous for the overloaded boats to attempt to rescue. The cause of the disaster still loomed in the distance.

At last the dawn and with it the debris strewn sea. Very soon we saw our rescuer the Carpathia and in a short time we were taken onboard and given stimulants and dry clothing of various shapes and sizes. Mother and I still thought that father had been picked up and the Americans treated us with much kindness and generosity.

We came back to the Union at the end of 1912, and my mother, who had not yet recovered from the shock, was advised by her doctor to take a long sea voyage. I thought we had had quite our fair share of the sea for some time to come. Mother took his advice and we had a trip to Australia and back.

In 1917 I met my future husband in Johannesburg and by a remarkable coincidence I discovered shortly after the disaster the Johannesburg Evening Chronicle had run a competition for a better method of saving life at sea. My husband won the competition.

Robert Hichens, the quartermaster of the Titanic, who was on the wheel when she struck, was also in Johannesburg and knew my husband very well.

Several years later, whilst living in Southampton, I frequently saw the Olympic, the Titanic's sister ship sail, and I noticed the greatly increased life saving equipment onboard.

As is known, out of a total of 2,200 passengers and crew, only 700 odd were saved, which meant that over 1,500 went to their doom. I think that in Southampton, where most of the crew came from, about 1,000 families were bereaved.

Little did I anticipate on that April day in 1912 that I should spend so many years in Southampton, from 1920 to 1943 and eventually become a mother to eight sons and two daughters.

Neither did I expect to see the town bombed, blasted and burnt as it *had been, and although the children and I went through it all, I felt no fear. However, my sea voyaging was not over, for early in 1944, I sailed to South Africa with six of my children and although we had two alerts on the way out, we arrived safely in Cape Town on February the 4th 1944.*

Four of my sons are at sea, three in the Royal Navy and one in the merchant service, and all went through the tough parts of the war at sea.

The above interview was held at their home in Simonstown when Edith was 51 years of age. Although there are a few discrepancies, editorial and otherwise, it is basically correct. There have been many other important interviews with Edith throughout her lifetime; I've included a few in the interest of showing how this type of disaster was described in that period.

Those five years of living in Simonstown made it hard to believe, especially for the younger children that there was a war going on. Life appeared to be good for all age groups. There was always plenty of outdoor activity for the kids, including swimming and mountain climbing. It was generally a good, full life for youngsters. They had a wide range of friends, some of them in school. Others were not permitted to attend a whites-only school, but nevertheless, they all got on well together. Many Malay fishermen took them along on short fishing trips, and they could never forget catching mackerel, snoek, and yellowtail. Sometimes they would be invited into their homes afterwards. There was a colour bar in those days under the General Smuts regime, but nothing like the apartheid to follow under later governments.

The 'bug hutch' was their local cinema, referred to as the bioscope. With segregation in force, there was an upstairs balcony for blacks; the whites sat downstairs in the stalls. Throughout the performances on Saturday mornings, missiles would be flung about the place, and there was an unending squeaking of seats, giggles, and shouts, along with the odd crisp bag being blown up and exploded.

They loved the place and always looked forward to their next visit to see Flash Gordon, Roy Rogers, Laurel and Hardy, or a wide range of Walt Disney classics. Away from the cinema, a Great Dane could be seen from time to time accompanying a sailor or two along the street. For reasons unknown, this dog followed sailors everywhere. Apparently, the owner became fed up with forever looking for the animal and eventually finding it roaming around the dockyard, so he offered it to the Royal Navy as a mascot. They decided that they could do with a mascot, signed him up to become able seaman nuisance, and set aside an allowance for him.

When the dog died many years later, he was buried with full naval honours at Klava Camp, on top of the mountain overlooking Simons Bay. To this day, his grave is well maintained, and a visit to Simonstown Museum will provide a detailed account of his life in the town.

The two youngest boys used to have chameleons at home, as did several other households. They loved to watch them on a cord stretched across the room, changing colour to suit their environment and catching flies and insects with their long, sticky tongues. Other things they would always remember were the wonderful local fruits and delicacies like prickly pears, figs, and biltong (beef jerky). They had been good years for them all, but like all good things, they eventually come to an end. During that period in South Africa, Premier Jan Smuts lost his seat to the Nationalist Party after 24 years in office. This ultimately brought about many changes in that country. They were not to notice those changes, however. The time had finally arrived for the Admiralty to start sending their staff back to the UK as they started to wind down their operations at the base. Fredrick's posting was coming to an end, and with it, so were the good times that many of them would look back on fondly.

On returning to Southampton in 1948, they sailed from Cape Town on Union Castle Line's *Pretoria Castle* on her maiden return voyage. They left behind the three sons serving in the Royal Navy and the eldest daughter, who had married a sailor whilst in Simonstown. Up to that point in time, the *Pretoria Castle* was the largest ship the children had ever set eyes on. Before boarding, they took in the great lavender hull, the white superstructure, and the massive red-and-black topped funnel. They sailed at 4 p.m. that day, leaving behind four members of the family, whom they wouldn't see again for several years. The children left behind many school friends, whom they would never see again. They were to learn later that on the *Pretoria Castle's* launching ceremony in 1947, Mrs Jan Smuts, the wife of the South African prime minister at the time, activated the actual launching from her home in Pretoria, some 6,000 miles away from Belfast. At the appointed time, she pressed a button, and the launching mechanism was activated by radio waves.

CHAPTER TWELVE

HOUNDWELL PARK

Edith had sailed from Cape Town many times before, and one can only imagine what must have gone through her mind as she saw Table Mountain once again fading away astern as the *Pretoria Castle* headed north into the Atlantic Ocean. Some ten days later, they arrived and dropped anchor off of Funchal, the capital of Madeira. It was fascinating to see all the little bumboats gathering around the ship as they dropped anchor. Local swimmers would go to the upper decks and, after collecting money to perform their feats, would dive from the highest points on deck into the deep blue water below. Others would go one better than that by diving into the water and then swimming right under the ship, coming up on the other side, grinning and waving to those watching from the upper decks. This was no mean feat, as a ship of 28,000 tons had a draught of some twenty-six feet, along with a beam, all of eighty feet, so top marks to them for their prowess.

The voyage from Madeira to Southampton took just a little over four days, and most of the family members were looking forward to arriving back in England. As the days went by, a few landmarks were visible, such as Cape Finisterre on the north-western tip of Spain and, later, another landfall, which was Northern France. Early on a Friday morning they docked in Southampton. Once off of the ship, Leo, the fourth-eldest son, and his wife met them to take them to their prefabricated home for a temporary stay.

Prefabs, as they were known in those days, were prefabricated dwellings built to ease the housing shortage and were suited to house a family of five. There were eleven of them cramped up in that small building, and it was hard going for all concerned. This was a far cry from the spacious home they had left back in Simonstown, and from here on in, they were all in for a rude awakening. The situation was desperate, but after just a couple of months something turned up and they were able to move out, giving Leo and his family some long-awaited space and freedom again.

Their new home was to be hut, a Nissen hut, in fact, situated in parkland in the centre of Southampton. This was an American military camp that was occupied by US servicemen and women during the war but had now been vacated. The dwellings were tunnel-shaped structures with corrugated iron roofs, wooden floorboards, and plywood partitions between each room. Each partition stopped some eighteen inches short of the roof in each room, resulting in privacy that was somewhat limited. The living space was in the front of the hut, which had a circular, coke-burning stove in the centre of the room and a chimney pipe going straight up through the roof. There were hardly any alterations made when the local authority took them over to ease the homeless problem.

There were about seventy-five of those dwellings, surrounded by an iron check wire fence about eight feet high, with one side looking out on the town's cricket pitches. The other side of the camp, as it was generally known, bordered a park. There was a main road on the other side of the fence. This, then, was to be their home for the next two years, and at times it brought Edith to tears.

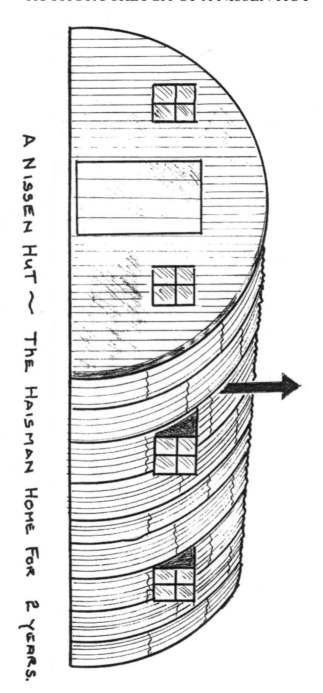

A NISSEN HUT ~ THE HAISMAN HOME FOR 2 YEARS.

Fredrick and Edith were to start another home in battle-scarred Southampton with bomb sites, ruins, and derelict buildings scattered around the empty streets. The whole camp, as it was known, was a part of town that most people would want to steer clear of, as there was always trouble with the police. The stove inside of the hut heated the main room quite well, but the rest of the hut remained very cold unless paraffin lamps could be placed in each bedroom. Sometimes, the cold was more bearable than the stink from paraffin fumes and it was worth going without that extra heat. Although they all hated the place, there just wasn't anywhere else to live. They would have to wait it out like everyone else until other accommodation became available.

Life in those huts was an education in itself. The residents were a real mixed bag, ranging from ordinary, decent folk to some real down-and-out types, with the odd prostitute or two. Police were regular visitors to Houndwell Park, to use its proper name at that time, and knew several of the residents by their first names. This was the first time they had seen women in stand-up fights, pulling at each other's hair and ripping each other's clothes off to cheers from onlookers. They witnessed fights between men and some terrible rows between neighbours. Most of it appeared to be over the kids and the trouble they got into. On Saturday mornings during the winter months, there would be a mass exodus of kids and grown-ups alike, pushing old prams or anything with wheels on it. They were heading for the gas works in order to pick up sacks of coke for the stoves and fireplaces in their homes. This was the cheapest way to get fuel, as delivery was more costly. One full sack would usually last until the following week, when they would all repeat the performance.

Toward the end of the decade and the beginning of the '50s, the rebuilding of Southampton was under way. It was a mammoth task, with a great deal of High Street having been heavily bombed during the war. One of the major changes to take place was the removal of the old tramlines, which included those that ran down The Avenue and along High Street. Those tramlines were laid on blocks of wood, a bit bigger than the size of a house brick. They were soaked in creosote and treated with tar and made an excellent source of fuel for the home fires. As the tramlines were lifted and the tar blocks, as they were known, were being dug up, there would be a never-ending stream of kids and adults pushing anything on wheels to carry those precious wooden blocks home. They were indeed precious to everyone for three very good reasons. Firstly, they were free. Secondly, with them, there was no need to buy coke from the gas works. Thirdly, each tar block would burn for hours in the types of stoves they had in their huts and provide really good heat. Practically the whole of the Houndwell Park population was involved in carting those valuable blocks home and storing them under their huts for a good supply of winter fuel.

During the Haisman family's stay at the huts in Southampton, the second-youngest son, Brian, was becoming too much for Edith to look after, as he was approaching 14 years of age. Although she insisted that she could care for him, he was just too much for her. He was almost twice her size and needed full-time care. Eventually she gave in, and he was finally taken into care. For a time, Edith was satisfied that perhaps she had done the right thing. She would visit him every week, and he appeared settled and quite content with his surroundings.

Suddenly, without warning, they learned that Brian had passed away one night from heart failure. Edith was devastated. She had nursed him throughout his life, and for it to end like it did left her shocked and heartbroken for a very long time. He was a beautiful boy and dearly loved by the whole family.

Living in those Nissen huts must have been a bitter experience for both parents after Simonstown. The younger ones soon adapted to their environment and got out and about with the other local children. It was a miserable place in the winter months, especially during foggy times, when the stink from many of the huts' stoves could be smelled everywhere. Many residents must have used their pot belly stoves as incinerators. The stench of burning rags, rubbish, and just about everything else that was combustible permeated the area, and foggy conditions made it much worse.

.At the beginning of the 1950s, everything was still rationed. At the grocer or sweet shop, they would have to hand over their ration books. The shopkeeper would then cut out the number of points allocated for each item from the book with a pair of scissors. The younger members of the family had friends with fathers in the merchant navy who would bring home Yankee comics and bubble gum. They would bargain and swap all kinds of things to get their hands on those popular items.

One morning before going to school, the residents noticed that all the menfolk going to work were being stopped by the police before being allowed to carry on to where they were going. It wasn't long before it was heard that a woman had been murdered during the night on a park bench just outside of the perimeter fence. The whole place was swarming with police that day, mainly because of the reputation the place had and the many unsavoury characters living there. It was learned later that the dead woman was a prostitute who apparently had an argument with a man late that night. The man had beat her up. Realising that he had gone too far, he dragged her body out to the middle of the cricket pitch. Much later that morning, he walked into the Southampton police station to give himself up.

After two long years, notice came through from the local authority that a new home had been found for the Haisman family at Bitterne, a suburb of Southampton. Everyone felt relief, more so Fredrick and Edith, at getting away from that place and being able to start living in a real home again.

This was a move that was to last for fifteen years, and perhaps Fredrick and Edith were as happy there as anywhere else they had lived. During that time all their children had left school and pursued their own lives. John and Donald chose the Royal Air Force as a career, whereas the youngest, David, chose a life in the merchant navy. Fredrick had left the Admiralty and joined John I. Thorneycroft's shipyard at Woolston in Southampton as an engineering draughtsman. The long spell of rationing had ended in 1954, and for a while everyone went mad buying chocolate and confectionary. It was Edith's favourite pastime.

In the late 1940s and early '50s, Southampton was a busy and interesting port. It had been quoted that between 4,000 and 5,000 seaman passed through the port each week in those days, and that was considered a conservative estimate. When one recalls the many troopships, emigrant ships, Union Castle Line, Royal Mail Line, Cunard Line, P&O line, Elders & Fyffes, and many other operators using the port on a regular basis, it becomes quite easy to see how those figures were arrived at. The Queen liners, for instance, with crews of well over 1,000 each, were arriving and sailing each week. The weekly arrivals of the other lines' ships, with crews of 500 or more, made it a port bustling with visiting seafarers of all nationalities.

In those days, one of the ideal vantage points in Southampton for seeing the great liners was the Royal Pier, which jutted out on the waterfront between the Old and New Docks. Although there was a pier toll to be paid, some of the youngsters knew how to get around that little handicap by mastering a few balancing and trapeze-style acts along the lower support stringers beneath the pier. As some of these huge liners passed by the pier head, with their tug boats fussing about them in readiness to nurse them alongside of their berths, it would be a fascinating scene for ship lovers.

On one particular day, many would witness the sailing of the 45,000-ton *Aquitania* on her final voyage to the breaker's yard in Scotland. On sailing, a bugler high up on the boat deck housing played the 'Last Post' as her Cunard White Star house flags were lowered for the last time.

This ship had been a wonderful old servant for the Cunard White Star Line, appearing similar to the Olympic-class liners and built a couple of years after *Titanic*. It was completing some thirty-five odd years of service for the company. This final sailing of the *Aquitania* was of special interest to Fredrick and Edith, as their fourth-eldest son, Leo, had signed on that ship as a bellboy in 1936, despite a great deal of persuasion from Edith not to do so. As a *Titanic* survivor herself, she remembered vividly how all the bellboys had drowned, and she repeatedly reminded him to check out where his lifeboat station was before unpacking his sea bag.

Other regular callers on the North Atlantic run during the 1950s were the U.S. Lines' *Manhattan* and her sister ship, *Washington*, which would soon be taken out of service and replaced by the U.S. Lines' *United States*. On entering service during her maiden voyage in 1952, the *United States* took the Blue Riband from the *Queen Mary* for the fastest Atlantic crossing after she had held that record for almost twenty years. Along with these regular visitors were the US troop transports, arriving and leaving berth 107 in the New Docks en route to Germany or returning to the US.

During January of 1953, a British Rail car ferry called the *Princess Victoria* sank in the Irish Sea with a loss of 128 people. After Edith had heard about this tragedy on the news and then read about it in the national press, she again pleaded with her youngest son, David, to think of something else other than going away to sea. Fredrick, on the other hand, thought the sea life was good for all young men. Those sentiments reflected his own boyhood, when he, too, wanted desperately to go to sea. It was understandable coming from Edith, as her own experiences had been enough to last her for a lifetime, and not forgetting her elder sons in the Royal Navy and how close two of them came to being lost at sea.

Knowing her children the way she did, she knew that they would make up their own minds, and the sea appeared to be in the blood of several of her sons. She had tried to deter other sons from going away to sea over the years, but this seemed to be a waste of time. She always knew that with Fredrick's positive approach to life at sea, it would have fallen on deaf ears.

CHAPTER THIRTEEN

V0YAGE OF REMEMBERANCE

On 17 July 1962, the premier showing of the film *A Night to Remember* was being held at the Odeon Cinema in Southampton and Edith, along with a few other *Titanic* survivors, was invited to attend. It was a fitting venue for the film, as Captain Rostron of the *Carpathia*, *Titanic's* rescue ship, opened the cinema back in 1937. Among those attending that evening were Bert Dean, Eva Hart, Milvina Dean, and Fred Fleet. From this time onward, Edith became good friends with other survivors, especially Milvina Dean. Together they attended many functions held by the various *Titanic* societies. Milvina Dean was just a babe in arms when the ship sank and naturally remembered nothing of the disaster. As a result, she always listened to Edith's experiences and what she had to say when answering questions from interested parties or the media. There's no doubt that she learned a great deal from Edith about what life was like for a teenager on the *Titanic*.

When asked over the years how she enjoyed the film, Edith always replied that it was probably the nearest any film had ever gotten to the truth of the actual disaster. Navigating officers from the *Titanic*, who may well have been expected to command their own ships in years to come, never achieved their goals. Shipping companies considered it bad publicity to have one of their ships commanded by an ex-*Titanic* officer, and the men would have to live with this for the rest of their lives.

Fredrick finally retired from Thorneycroft's shipyard and was toying with the idea of retiring out in Australia. He and Edith had a son and a daughter who had already settled there with their families, and Fredrick thought they had nothing to lose. Edith was a little more reluctant to sell up another home and move abroad. She had done so several times in the past and was, for all intents and purposes, reasonably well settled at their home in Bitterne. It could be said that Edith had suffered in silence on many occasions. She never considered the move to be a wise one at their age, but she would always go along with the flow regarding her family.

In December 1964, Fredrick and Edith sailed from Southampton on the P&O liner *Oriana*, arriving in Brisbane on 14 January 1965. On their arrival in Australia, they were met by their son and daughter. They received quite a bit of publicity due to Edith's connection with the *Titanic*. Other members of the family began to follow them to Australia, looking for a better life, and several of them are still there to this day.

EDITH AND FREDRICK MEET THEIR GRANDAUGHTER IN AUSTRALIA

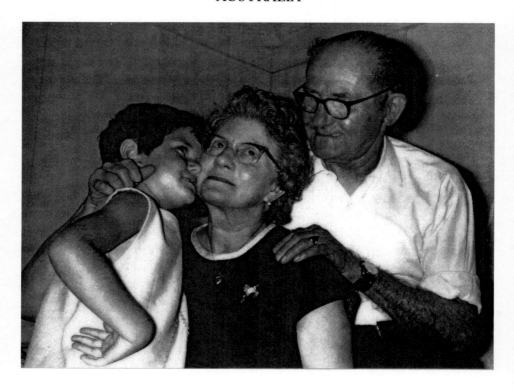

After five years, Fredrick wanted to return to England. Edith was expecting it, knowing him the way she did. She knew that her husband had a particularly conservative outlook on life and, ultimately, there was no place like England to spend the rest of his days. They arrived back in Southampton in the winter of 1969 on a bitterly cold day and in the middle of a power strike. Edith was 74 at that time, and Fredrick was two years older. Together, they had to start all over again. They finally managed to get an elderly person's flat in Westwood Road in Portswood, Southampton that, by coincidence, was the next road to Winn Road, where Captain Smith of the *Titanic* had lived until sailing from Southampton on that fateful voyage.

The flat they occupied was warden-controlled, and once again they were settled. They had a good few visits each week from family and friends. The *Titanic* was just a memory, with no one ever speaking about it other than when a survivor passed on. In 1977, they celebrated their diamond wedding anniversary at Rhinefield House in the New Forest. Rhinefield House was a beautiful, stately home in the heart of the forest and, although privately owned, part of it could be hired for private occasions. It was a grand occasion, with all the family and relations as far afield as Australia attending the function. They dined in medieval style, with jugs of mead and glasses of wine brought by serving wenches in front of roaring log fires. It was a celebration worthy of a couple who had been married for sixty years, had ten children, and travelled across the world together. A tree was planted for them in the grounds of the flats where they lived, with the lord mayor of Southampton attending a garden party held in the grounds for the residents there.

A couple of months after their anniversary celebrations, Fredrick became ill. Edith was determined that she was going to look after him, even though it was too much for her. He was eventually taken to hospital, an experience he had never endured throughout his life. Once admitted, he suffered a stroke and passed away a few days later, on 26 November of that same year. Edith was heartbroken, having lost her partner through life for sixty years. Although the family did their best to console her, they were never to know the grief she felt. She was 81 years of age and would face the time left to her alone in her flat at Portswood. As a strong-willed woman, she was determined to carry on and remain physically independent for as long as possible. All she ever wanted was for the family to continue to visit her on a regular basis. They did this much as before, although they now took it in turns to pop in every day.

On 5 December 1980, Edith learned of the death of her eldest son, Fredrick, Jr., in London. He had died from heart disease, aged just 62. This news was totally unexpected and came as a great shock to Edith, as it was to all of the rest of them. He had clearly kept his illness to himself for some considerable time, as they were to confirm later.

In 1981, serious attempts were being made to search the depths of the North Atlantic to find the sunken wreck of the *Titanic*. Edith learned of the attempts from her youngest son. She said at the time that they would never find it and that the ship had gone forever. Searches by the US Navy continued in the area, mainly because they wanted to try out new submersible equipment in great depths of water.

By 1984, the Americans had teamed up with the French and carried out further extensive searches in a large area thought to be where the ship had gone down. On the 1st of September an echo was received by sounding gear, believed to be that of a boiler casing. After further sweeps in the area it was confirmed that, after seventy-two years, the *Titanic* had finally been found. The location of the wreck some two miles below the surface caused a great deal of excitement and enormous public interest. When the find of the *Titanic* was put to Edith, she was absolutely amazed. She wanted to know what on earth they were going to do with it. She was told that the wreck was too deep and nothing could be done. She appeared satisfied with that answer and said the dead should be left to rest in peace.

Unfortunately, that was not to be. The finding of the wreck began to stir up ideas in those who could see great advantages coming from this find. The quiet life Edith had enjoyed over the past few years was about to change dramatically, as some people began to view her with renewed interest. Gone were those little chats with friends and relatives from time to time about the *Titanic*. Now they wanted her autograph. More and more people were seeking her out to get her to sign bits of paper or anything that could be written on.

Dr Robert Ballard, heading the expedition, had said that the ship was lying in 13,000 feet of water and was in total darkness and at peace. On discovery of the vessel, they held a service on board for those who had perished at that place seventy-two years ago. A brass plate was placed on the wreck of the *Titanic* for those who had lost their lives, and Doctor Ballard was of the opinion that the wreck should remain in peace, the way she had been for all those years. Edith felt comforted to know that the dead were being respected and thought, like many others, that there would no longer be any interference with the ship.

In August 1985, Edith and the remaining family were to hear of the death of John, the sixth-eldest son, from cancer, aged just 54. It was another shock for everyone who knew him, as this man led a perfectly healthy life and one would have expected him to have a long life ahead of him.

By 1986, another expedition was carried out on the *Titanic* wreck site. Manned dives in a submersible were made on the ship. On several of these dives, a small, remote-controlled pod fitted with cameras was operated from inside of the submersible and, for the first time in seventy-four years, the inside of the *Titanic* could be seen. There were to follow amazing pictures of wreckage and the ship's fittings scattered around the ocean floor. The ship itself had settled on an almost even keel, with its bow buried deep in the mud. The stern section lay almost half a kilometre away from the forward section, confirming that the ship had broken her back and had parted during sinking. The impact on the ocean floor was evident by the collapsed decks on the stern section and the buckled hull plates on her forward section.

Some pictures had shown that her huge reciprocating engines and cylinders had come off better, standing almost upright amidst the wreckage. Between the two sections lay a vast debris field with numerous pieces of crockery, deck fittings, suitcases, the odd safe, bottles of wine, and large quantities of coal from the ship's bunkers. Brass fittings around the portholes, windows, and capstan tops, along with the bronze propellers, stood the test of time. They will probably be the last bits of *Titanic* that will remain visible for years to come. All wooden fitments had disappeared, although, quite surprisingly, some leather goods remained intact, as did clothing folded up in suitcases, which were later brought to the surface by salvage teams. There was never any sign of human remains, as was first thought. This was probably due to the great pressure and the organisms that will eventually destroy everything that was once *Titanic*. For those carrying out the restoration work, it was obviously an exciting time, but Edith and many relatives of *Titanic* survivors thought that all those things should have been left well alone.

THE AUTHOR AND HIS WIFE WITH THOMAS'S POCKET WATCH

On 15 April 1987, the seventy-fifth anniversary of the sinking of the *Titanic* was observed. Edith and one or two of the last survivors were flown out to America to attend a 'Historical Titanic Convention.' It was also during that year that no less than 2,000 items were retrieved from the wreck, including Thomas's gold pocket watch, taken from a Gladstone bag along with $60,000 dollars, and claimed by the salvage company. As the publicity increased, Edith was invited to more and more functions, although by then she was wheelchair-bound. Those organising the functions said she enjoying them, but by that time, in her mid-nineties, she was also becoming extremely tired of it all as well.

In 1993, Edith was presented with her father's gold pocket watch during a function at the Hilton Hotel in Southampton. She was brought to tears to think that, at long last, she had something from her father, and she clearly believed it to be his watch. Her family went along with that throughout the rest of her life and wouldn't spoil it for all the tea in China. However, her family knew for a fact that the watch was destined for Edith's stepbrother and was engraved on the back, but they were never allowed to see the inscription, as it remained fixed in a presentation box. Whoever has that watch today should not advertise it as belonging to Edith until certain remaining members of Edith's family can examine the engraving and confirm that it is indeed Thomas's watch.

In 1995, Edith received an invitation from the owners of the wreck at that time, R.M.S. Titanic.inc. to go on a short cruise to the *Titanic* site. Edith and her daughter Dorothy flew to America and joined a ship called the *Island Breeze* with a few dignitaries and the last one or two survivors. Edith had finally set sail on her last ocean voyage, heading for a position in the North Atlantic marked on a chart as 41 46' N 50 14' W. On reaching this position on the ocean, the *Island Breeze* stopped. Below them lay the wreck of the *Titanic*, in darkness and at peace. Edith, now wheelchair-bound, attended a service, which was held on the open deck, for the 1,500 souls who had perished at that place eighty-four years ago. The memories of the nightmare of 15 April 1912 came flooding back to her. A lone piper played a lament high on the upper decks as she was helped to the ship's rail. Peering down, she let a wreath fall from her hands to the dark waters below in memory of her dear father. She was overcome and wept silently as she again thought of how her father must have fought for his life in those icy waters of the North Atlantic.

It had always been her lifelong desire to pay her last respects to her dear departed father, and now, eighty-four years later, her life's dream had been achieved. She had finally carried it out.

On 27 October 1996, Edith received a telegram from the Queen congratulating her on her one hundredth birthday. The celebrations were held at the Hilton Hotel in Southampton, and well-wishers came from many parts, including America and Australia. One of the guests was Princess Elletra Marconi, the daughter of the radio pioneer. Without his invention, it would be difficult to imagine just how few would have survived the *Titanic* disaster.

In 1996, Edith and the remaining family were to hear of the death of Kenneth, the second eldest son, who died from Alzheimer's disease.

On 20 January 1997, at 7.30 p.m., Edith passed away quietly in her sleep after suffering from pneumonia. She left behind four sons, two daughters, and forty grandchildren. She had outlived her husband and four of her own children. She had been born into a wealthy family and, one could imagine, would have had a good future to look forward to. However, the sinking of the *Titanic* had mapped out an entirely different life for her. She was to live a life of giving, and she gave all she had, never asking for anything in return. Destiny had decided that she would go on her long journey through life without wealth. Instead, she would leave a better legacy to those she left behind: her love, her courage, and her resilience. If her mother and father could have witnessed the way their brave little daughter had gone through life, they would never have believed it.

To her sons and daughters, she was not only a wonderful mother but also a marvellous human being. She has left them all proud at being part of her life.

ABOUT THE AUTHOR

Edith Haisman (ne'e Brown), up until her death in January 1997, was the world's oldest living survivor of the *Titanic* disaster, the author, David, being her youngest son. He has travelled the world for many years, serving for thirty years in the British merchant service in the capacity of able seaman, quartermaster, mate, and skipper on coastal tankers.

In 1955, he joined Cunard White Star Line, as it was then known, and sailed on two of the world's greatest liners at that time, namely the *Queen Mary* and the *Queen Elizabeth*, as able seaman/lookout man. Those voyages to New York were over the same course the *Titanic* took, and he experienced the very same conditions. He later joined other ships of the line, the *Ascania,* the *Mauretania*, and the *Saxonia*. On the Canadian run, it was sometimes necessary to stop at night in the middle of vast ice fields and wait for daybreak before proceeding into the St Lawrence Seaway. During those times, he would try to imagine what it must have been like for his mother, cramped up in a small lifeboat in freezing conditions.

His experience and first-hand knowledge of ships in the very same conditions gives his account greater credibility than most writers on the subject. While compiling his mother's life story, the author drew upon his years of personal experience sailing on these great ships and his knowledge of the port of Southampton.

Living in Southampton, he had spoken many times to Fred Fleet, the lookout man on the *Titanic* who had first spotted the iceberg. Fleet was a newspaper seller in the city and was known by many seamen in the port. He had been an orphan, and he ended his sea career in 1936.

Later, after falling on hard times and losing his wife, he took his own life in 1965.

Throughout her life, the author's mother had told her family vivid stories of that fateful night of 14 April 1912. She was fifteen years old at the time and could well remember the terrifying cries for help as literally hundreds of men, women, and children were dying in the icy waters of the North Atlantic. Those sounds were to haunt her for the rest of her life.

In this story, the author has taken the liberty to comment on some of the working practices that, in his view, caused much unnecessary hardship for those working within the industry at the time of the *Titanic* and in the ensuing years.

Throughout this story, nautical terms have been kept to a minimum. Where they are used, they are in today's terminology for simplicity.

The end

Breinigsville, PA USA
12 May 2010
237856BV00001B/25/P